THE CONNOISSEUR NEW GUIDE TO

Antique English

POTTERY, PORCELAIN
AND GLASS

Edited by L. G. G. Ramsey, Editor of *The Connoisseur*

With an Introduction by G. Bernard Hughes

E. P. DUTTON & COMPANY, INC., NEW YORK

Designed and produced for E. P. DUTTON & CO., INC.
by Rainbird, McLean Ltd, 11 Charlotte Street, London W1
First Published in the U.S.A., 1961 by E. P. Dutton & Co., Inc.

© The Connoisseur 1961

Printed in England

Contents

Introduction

Almost four centuries ago William Harrison marvelled at the "pots of earth of sundry colours" on the rich Englishman's table and the glassware that even the poorest were beginning to demand. Yet in the light of subsequent history the collector sees such refinements as but an introductory phase to the story of English pottery, porcelain and glass. The purpose of this book is to present that story as an integrated pattern. It is divided sectionally for convenience into the accepted periods of English history, but demonstrates throughout both the perpetual changes and developments contained within any period and the sweep of advance that ignores the hazards of monarchy or politics.

It has been prepared for the lover of old china and glass who appreciates each detail of structure and pattern, and for the student of social history who understands the underlying significance of changes in fickle fashion. But especially it is for the collector, who may look for some chronological sequence to his chance acquisitions and for the guidance that will enable him to seek wisely and bargain shrewdly for further prizes.

The story is indeed fascinating. Little enough is known of medieval ceramics and only in Tudor days did earthenware find a place on the Englishman's table. Glass, made in England under Roman occupation, became a manufacture of consequence again only after about 1570. Even in William Harrison's Elizabethan England the commoners' plates and bowls were ill-glazed and far from impervious to stains, the mugs and beakers rough to the lips unless rimmed in silver or pewter; the home-produced greenish glass was flawy and perilously fragile. Already, however, imports from abroad were suggesting the pattern of things to come. Exquisite Chinese porcelains and ornately delicate Venetian glass remind the student of this eager, turbulent period that here was the challenge to native craftsmen and here may be found the roots of design and manufacturing techniques that have developed in England without serious interruptions to late Victorian days. Indeed, just because the more recent periods of Regency and Victorian have left a disproportionately vast aggregation of possible specimens, it is peculiarly important for the serious collector to make the comprehensive survey set out within this book.

Among the subjects under review it is seldom possible to attribute an exact date: all too rarely, even, can a maker be identified. But an immense amount of pleasure and satisfaction may be obtained from the alignment of a specimen with the various details of design, material and manufacturing technique that constituted the vogue—for a decade, perhaps, or even for a single year.

Design must depend upon social custom, upon fashions in wining and dining, upon tastes in furnishing and ornament, upon the whole concept of good living, expressed, for example, in such a small but conspicuous detail as the changing purpose of that commonest vessel, the saucer. For a study of custom affecting design the collector may consider the glass flutes evolved for champagne when that drink's slight sediment affronted the fastidious. The collector of champagne glasses may well study the whole history of the drink to understand his tazzas, flutes and coupes. Yet these elegant vessels are only a few of the Stuart and Georgian glasses whose charming designs reflect their roles in custom and etiquette, telling the discerning collector of punch parties, or teatime cordials, or the lavish gaiety of the informal dessert.

No less important in determining the lineage of a specimen is the question of its material. Great care has been used throughout this volume to offer illustrations that do justice to the surface texture and ornament of these wares. Here the story of ceramics covers the range of opaque earthenwares, of more austere stonewares and, from the 1740's, of various "soft paste" and "hard paste" imitations of Oriental porcelain which culminated, quantitatively, in the nineteenth-century development of the cheaper sturdier and wholly English ceramic bone china. Such distinction, of course, is far too sweeping: in particular the nineteenth-century potters developed many extremely fine bodies and pastes including, for instance, the now-fashionable marble imitation known as parian ware. But as indication of the collector's concern in changes of material it may be enough to cite the development of Wedgwood's cream-coloured earthenware and finer, whiter pearlware from 1780. This was a direct result of his breaking a monopoly covering ingredients he needed, a monopoly that impeded the progress of porcelain manufacture for a further fourteen years, when at last bone china could be developed.

To the glass collector the great change in materials came with the English development of flint glass from 1675. But every stage of the story reflects the burden of glass taxes, until their abolition in 1845 released the spectacular brilliance of English coloured glass described in the chapter on Early Victorian glass, ranging from gaudy novelties to exquisite millefiori paperweights.

Regarding the part played by advances in technique, the collector of old glass can observe with particular clarity man's gradual mastery of this difficult metal. It is sufficient here, perhaps, to mention that the great improvements in cut ornament, early and late in the eighteenth century, were directly due to advances in the technique of annealing or toughening the glass. The result may be seen in the splendid cut glass illustrating the surveys of the Georgian and Regency periods

The lover of English ceramics may base his collection on such an important technique as the ornament achieved by transfer printing. He can trace the development of this work through the early stages of heavy blurred outlines and cross-hatched shadows to the delicate outlines prepared for hand colouring. He can range endlessly among some of the loveliest and most varied ceramics still available for private collection, grouped under the general term "Staffordshire blue".

In the foregoing paragraphs a few possible fields of interest for the collector have been suggested. But among ceramics as among glassware the opportunities for the alert collector are limitless. Granted he must possess that indescribable flair which leads him to bargains where others have looked in vain. Yet the main prerequisites for success are the sense of period, the awareness of style and texture, the eye for shape and ornament which come only from study of authenticated specimens and of the society that brought them into being, and the instinctive, intense affection that gives purpose and delight to the hobby of collecting antiques.

G. Bernard Hughes

POTTERY AND
PORCELAIN

TUDOR

Lead-glazed wares. The characteristic medieval pottery of England was lead-glazed earthenware of plain red or buff clay, the glaze either brown or yellow in tone, or stained a leaf-green by the addition of copper. These green-glazed wares were taken up and improved during the Tudor period, to become perhaps the most characteristic indigenous pottery of the sixteenth century, at least in the south-eastern parts of England. The most notable development of the period was in the direction of an all-round refinement. For the body a whitish clay was used, on which the green glaze, itself improved in depth of colour and in brilliance, showed up to far greater advantage. This improvement in quality was accompanied by a great extension of the forms for which pottery was used. The medieval pottery shape *par excellence* was the large jug. Such jugs, although they are known to have been ordered for Royal use, were probably employed only in the cellar and buttery. The actual table-furniture would be of other materials – wood, silver, horn or glass. With the Tudor period, pottery finds its way on to the table. Henry VIII had "green plates of earth for spice and fruit", and in the excavations of Eltham Palace during the 1930's there was found a green-glazed dish decorated with the Royal Arms supported by the dragon and greyhound – a version of the Arms which must antedate the accession of Queen Elizabeth I (Pl. 1c). This decoration is taken from a mould, while the rim of the dish is ornamented with a *guilloche* design freely incised with a pointed instrument. Comparable with this dish is a much-damaged flask in the British Museum. This bears moulded on one side the same coat-of-arms, which, taken in conjunction with other devices and the inscription DNE SALVVM FAC REGEM REGINAM ET REGNUM ("O Lord, save the King, the Queen and the Kingdom"), makes it virtually certain that the flask was made in the reign either of Henry VII or of Henry VIII. The same may be said of a fine cistern in the Victoria and Albert Museum decorated in moulded relief with the Royal Arms supported by the English lion and the Welsh griffin, as borne by Henry VII (Pl. 1A). This achievement is accompanied by the rose and lily and the initials H R and E R, for *Henricus Rex* and *Elisabetha Regina* (Elizabeth of York, consort of Henry VII). Flanking the ornaments already described are pilasters delicately moulded with a design of symmetrical plant-forms springing from a slender gadrooned urn, a characteristic motive of the Italian Renaissance. Any Renaissance influence on English art, however, is extremely rare before 1515, and almost unthinkable before 1509. It therefore seems more likely that the cistern was made after Henry VII's death, and probably as late as 1525 or 1530. The survival of the emblems of a previous reign can be paralleled in the windows of King's College Chapel, Cambridge, where the tracery-lights contain both the initials H E (Henry VII and Elizabeth) and H K (Henry VIII and Katherine of Aragon). Work did not begin on these windows until 1515 at the earliest.

The cistern just described is perhaps the most important surviving piece of Tudor pottery, but there are numerous other green-glazed pieces which are akin to it in that they bear the Royal Arms or initials and are themselves of a semi-architectural nature. These comprise wall-sconces to hold candles, and large hollow tiles and other components of glazed stoves of German type. The candle-sconces (one of which is traditionally said to have come from Hampton Court) bear the initials E R and may well be of the reign of Edward VI. If they are, they form, with the similarly decorated stove-tiles already referred to, a bridge between the cistern of Henry VIII's reign and other pieces which are indisputably of the Elizabethan period (such as a tile-fragment bearing the recognizable portrait of the Queen). These hollow stove-tiles, which are about $13\frac{1}{2}$ in. by 10 in. in size, have been found in a number of different places, a fact which suggests that tiled stoves of the sort familiar from Germany and Switzerland enjoyed a vogue in Tudor England. William Harrison, in his *Description of England*, written in 1577 and revised in 1587, says: "As for stoves, we have not hitherto used them greatly, yet do they now begin to be made in divers houses of the gentry and wealthy citizens … " Had such stoves remained in use in England, they would have provided a comfort for Englishmen the absence of which Lady Mary Wortley Montagu was to lament some two hundred years later. The fact that the custom was never established in England, and the close similarity between English and Continental tiles, suggest that they were manufactured by immigrant potters.

It is clear from what has been said above that green-glazed pottery was manufactured throughout the Tudor period, and that it had even found its way on to the royal table by Henry VIII's reign. It is not, however, so certain that its use in this way was widespread. In a description of an election feast of the Drapers' Company in 1522, occurs the passage: "At the said High board were … green pots of ale and wine, with ashen cups set before them at every mess; but they had gilt cups for red wine and ipocras." Here the "green pots" may have been jugs rather than drinking-vessels. In the records of the Inner Temple, however, occurs in 1559–60 the order: "that from henceforth there shall not any ashen cups be provided, but the House to be served in green cups, both of winter and summer". A number of fragments and complete pieces of green-glazed pottery have been found on the sites of the various Inns of Courts, and one now in the British Museum is mounted with a silver collar inscribed "Found in a Vault under the Steward's

Office, Lincoln's Inn, 1788" (Pl. 1B). These pots, being of too small capacity for jugs, must be the "green cups" of the Inner Temple records. Other table-wares in the same type of pottery include finely shaped lobed cups; circular saucer-dishes; and candlesticks (one of these is stamped with the Pegasus badge of the Inner Temple, Pl. 3B). Objects of humbler use include chafing-dishes; kitchen-mortars; feeding-dishes for chickens, formed of a series of concentric raised ridges; and tur-nip-shaped money-boxes, or "thrift-boxes", the subject of a popular conceit in the immediately succeeding period – as in Mason's *Handful of Essaies*, 1621: "Like a swine, he never doth good till his death; as an apprentice's box of earth, apt he is to take all, but to restore none till hee be broken."

In the excavation of the sites of several Yorkshire Cistercian abbeys at the end of the last century there were found numerous fragments of a hard pottery of dark-red body and an almost black, metallic glaze. From the circumstances of their finding, these wares were dubbed "Cistercian" wares, and they must in general date from before the Dissolution of the monasteries in 1540. A characteristic shape in this pottery was a tall mug of trumpet shape, with two handles ("tyg"), and it is a significant coincidence that the *Regulations of the Order of Cistercians of the Strict Observance* lay it down that: "Each religious has for his own use a wooden spoon and fork, a knife, a two-handled cup, and a napkin." This rule dates back at least to the early twelfth century. Mugs of this same form, however, continued to be made long after the Dissolution, as an example dated 1599 in the British Museum clearly proves (Pl. 3D). Some tygs found on the sites of the Yorkshire abbeys had four, or as many as eight, handles; and this multiplicity of handles remained a feature of English pottery right into the eighteenth century. Mugs of inverted bell-shape, with three handles, were made in the vicinity of Abergavenny, in Monmouthshire; and other potteries producing these hard, dark-glazed wares were situated at Babylon, near Ely; at Tickenhall in Derbyshire; at Wrotham in Kent, and possibly also in Bristol. Most of this pottery was plain (Pl. 3F), but occasional telling use was made of horizontal ribbing, and some of the Yorkshire (and possibly also the Tickenhall) wares were decorated with pads of white "slip" under the glaze (Pl. 3C, E). These were cut in the form of small roundels, rosettes or the like, and occasionally, as on a series of covered porringers from the monastic sites, formed into overall designs of different types.

Tin-glazed earthenware. One of the great inventions in the history of pottery was the discovery of a glaze suitable for decoration by means of painting. This was obtained by adding oxide (ashes) of tin to a lead glaze, thus providing a beauti-fully smooth and dense white surface. Originally discovered in the Near East as long ago as the ninth century A.D., it passed in the late fourteenth century, by way of Spain, to Italy. In the Italy of the High Renaissance, that forcing-ground of painters, painted pottery of this type ("maiolica") reached its zenith during the fifteenth and sixteenth centuries. The demand for maiolica in other parts of Europe ensured that the art of making it spread in the course of the sixteenth century to the Netherlands, the Germanic lands, France and England. The agents of this diffusion were usually migrant Italian potters. One of them, a certain Guido di Savino (of Castel Durante, in the duchy of Urbino), set up a pottery in Antwerp not later than 1512. In the Netherlands he was referred to as Guido Andries, and various members of his family were engaged in potting both in Antwerp and elsewhere. England at this time had very close connexions with the Netherlands, and a proportion at least of the Flemish "maiolica" of the early sixteenth century found its way to England, including perhaps some of the many pieces in Henry VIII's inventories described as "of gally-makynge" – an expression commonly used of tin-glazed pottery in the sixteenth and seventeenth centuries. A number of pieces dug up in London and elsewhere suggest by their style a Netherlands origin, and a series of tiles found in England undoubtedly came from the same source. It was no doubt this ready demand for Netherlands maiolica in England which encouraged two potters to come here at the time of the persecution of Protestants in the Netherlands after 1566. Stow's *Survey of the Cities of London and Westminster* (in Strype's edition of 1720) records: "About the Year 1567, Jasper Andries and Jacob Janson, Potters, came away from Antwerp, to avoid the Persecution there, & settled themselves in Norwich; where they followed their Trade, making Gally Paving Tiles, and Vessels for Apothecaries and others, very artificially. Anno 1570 they removed to London ...; & desired by Petition, from Queen Elizabeth, that they might have Liberty to follow their Trade in that City without Interruption; and presented her with a Chest of their Handy-work ..." Jasper Andries, who must have been related to Guido Andries, appears to have remained in East Anglia, but Jacob Janson settled in the Liberty of Catherine Creechurch in Aldgate, and appears to have attracted to himself a number of other potters of Flemish extraction. It was perhaps at this pottery that was made the only inscribed and dated piece of English "maiolica" which can be definitely attributed to the Tudor period – a dish in the London Museum bearing the inscription THE ROSE IS RED THE LEAVES ARE GRENE GOD SAVE ELIZABETH OUR QUEENE, and painted in blue, purple, green, orange and yellow with what may well be meant for a representation of the Tower of London hard by (Pl. 2C). This dish is dated 1600. A number of small cylindrical drug-jars (perhaps the "Vessels for Apothecaries" of Andries' Petition) and of bulbous-bodied jugs with cylindrical necks, apparently copying the contemporary Rhenish stonewares, may have been made, as well as found, in London. But it is naturally impossible at this period to distinguish between Flemish imports and pieces made in London by Flemings in their native style. There is, however, one class of wares which seems to be exclusively English. This comprises jugs of the bulbous-bodied type referred to above, often mounted in precious-metal mounts. The earliest dated example bears the London hall-mark for 1549–50 (Pl. 2B). These jugs are covered with a tin-glaze coloured blue or green, or dappled in tones of blue, purple, yellow, brown and green, in different combinations. A number of them have Kentish associations (the class as a whole is referred to as the "Malling" jugs, from the village of that name), and two examples which closely resemble them, but which have a mottled brown lead-glaze (Pl. 2A), have been regarded as the possible forerunners of the later pottery made at Wrotham, in the same county. Since two of the potters who joined Jacob Janson in Aldgate had previously been settled at Sandwich, a Kentish origin for this family is by no means out of the question. Of their English manufacture there can be no doubt.

Foreigners remarked of the English that they were wont to mount their cups in silver or silver-gilt. Thus, Stephen Perlin, a Frenchman, visiting England in 1558, writes: "They consume great quantities of beer, double and single, and do not drink it out of glasses, but from earthen pots with silver handles and covers, and this even in houses of persons of middling fortune; for as to the poor, the covers of their pots are only pewter ..." These silver-mounted cups no doubt formed part of the "garnish" of plate which a butler laid out on his "cupboard" (or sideboard) –

"than emperialle thy Cuppeborde [lay] with Silver & gild fulle gay".

A manuscript work of the late fifteenth or early sixteenth century, entitled "Ffor to serve a lord", lays down instructions for the due preparation of a banquet: "Thenne the boteler shall bryng forth basyns, ewers, and cuppis ... redressing all his silver plate, upon the cubbord, the largest firste, the richest in the myddis, the lightest before." This no doubt refers to silver cups, but a passage from William Harrison makes it clear that mounted pottery cups too were displayed on the "cupboard": "As for drink, it is usually filled in pots, goblets, jugs, bowls of silver in noblemen's houses; also in fine Venice glasses of all forms: and, for want of these elsewhere, in pots of earth of sundry colours and moulds, whereof many are garnished with silver, or at the leastwise with pewter, all which notwithstanding are seldom set on the table, but each one, as necessity urgeth, calleth for a cup of such drink as him listeth to have, so that, when he has tasted of it, he delivered the cup again to some one of the standers by, who, making it clean by pouring out the drink that remaineth, restoreth it to the cupboard from whence he fetched the same. By this device ... much idle tippling is furthermore cut off ..."

Examples of English pottery mounted in silver-gilt or pewter have already been quoted: of far greater moment than these indigenous wares, however, were the pottery and porcelain imported from abroad.

Chinese porcelain. Isolated examples of Chinese porcelain began to reach Europe in the fourteenth and fifteenth centuries, and are recorded as great treasures in the inventories of princes and potentates. It was probably not, however, until the Portuguese made direct contact with China, in 1514, that this precious commodity began to reach Europe in appreciable quantities: and of these, only a small proportion percolated to Northern Europe. When pieces of porcelain did come to England, they were naturally treated as great rarities, and were mounted in precious metal mounts, to be kept in treasuries or "cabinets of curiosities". New College, Oxford, possesses a small bowl of the grey-green Chinese porcelain known in latter days as "celadon", mounted in silver-gilt with broad bands round the rim and foot connected by openwork hinged straps (Pl. 4B). It was given to the College by Archbishop Warham, and although the mount is not dated, it must have been made not later than 1530, when the bowl was left to the College. The porcelain itself is probably considerably older. The earliest mounted piece with an English hall-mark is a small bowl in the David Foundation, University of London. It is of white porcelain with incised decoration on the outside, and on the inside painting in blue on the white ground. The silver-gilt mount bears the London date-letter for 1569–70. The decoration on the inside of this cup gives a foretaste of things to come; for from this date onwards, the porcelain *par excellence* for the European market was blue-and-white. It began to issue in considerable quantities in the course of the reign of the Chinese Emperor Wan Li (1573–1619). But the full exploitation of the European market did not occur until the seventeenth century was well under way. Numerous pieces of Wan Li blue-and-white porcelain with English silver or silver-gilt mounts are known, but of these the most famous are those which by a trustworthy tradition are reputed to have come from Burghley House, one of the seats of Lord William Cecil, Queen Elizabeth I's Lord Treasurer (Pl. 4A). The interest of the Cecil family in porcelain is confirmed by the list of New Year's gifts offered to the Queen in 1587–8. These include –

Item, one porrynger of white porselyn, garnished with gold, the cover of golde, with a lyon on the toppe therof; all geven by the Lord Threasorour, 38 oz.

Item, one cup of grene pursselyne, the foote, shanke, and cover silver guilte, chased lyke droppes. Geven by Mr Robert Cecill, 15 oz.

Item, one cup of pursseline, thone syde paynted red, the foote and cover sylver guilt. Geven by Mr. Lychfelde, 14 oz.qª.

A bowl of the type perhaps indicated by the last item is now in the collection of Judge Untermyer, in New York. The porcelain, probably of the Chia Ching period (1522–66), is coral-red on the outside, with a faint decoration of gold scrolls; whilst in the interior is a medallion enclosing chrysanthemums in underglaze blue (Pl. 5A). The mount probably dates from the 1570's. By the end of the century, porcelain had become sufficiently common to have passed beyond the prerogative of great lords. In 1599 the German traveller Thomas Platter remarked in the house of a certain Mr Cope, the owner of a cabinet of curiosities, "Earthen pitchers from China" and "Porcelain from China".

Chinese porcelain, along with other exotic rarities such as coconut-shells and ostrich-eggs, imperatively called for precious-metal mounts, both for protection and embellishment. So too did the gaily painted Turkish pottery of Isnik, of which a few pieces appear to have reached England in the course of the sixteenth century (Pl. 5B). Far less rare, but of considerable ceramic distinction, was the German salt-glazed stoneware. This stoneware was mainly manufactured in the Rhineland.

At Siegburg, near Bonn, was made a greyish ware of considerable charm, even when left unglazed, as was often the case. It was usually decorated with applied moulded relief-designs, but an effective technique of cutting a diaper pattern of interlocking lozenge-forms was also practised. Far more common than these wares in England, however, were those made at Cologne and later at the neighbouring Frechen. These, owing to the use of an iron-bearing clay, fired to a rich brown colour which shines most handsomely in a silver mount (Pl. 5c). The jugs most favoured in England during the second half of the sixteenth century were roughly globular in shape, with low footrim and short cylindrical neck, and a simple, strong strap-handle, to which the mounts of rim and cover were attached. It is possible that these were made especially for the English market. The jugs selected for mounting were commonly plain, and in this were chosen with great discrimination. Other jugs, however, were simply decorated with applied moulded reliefs – most frequently with the effigy of a bearded man applied below the neck in front. These are commonly called "Bellarmines" being supposedly made in derision of the Cardinal of that name, who, as a counter-Reformation controversialist, incurred the odium of Northern Europe. That they were referred to by contemporaries as "Bellarmines" is certain, since in Ben Jonson's play *The Ordinary* occurs the passage:

> Or like a larger jug that some men call
> A Bellarmine ...

The face on the front of the bottle must have taken on life in the wine-fevered fancy of many an English tippler, like the carouser in another play by Ben Jonson, *Bartholomew Fayre*, who had "wrashled so long with the bottle here, that the man with the beard hash almosht streck up hish heelsh".

German stoneware was certainly imported into England in considerable quantities during the sixteenth century, although by no means all of it was worthy of mounting in silver-gilt, some of the bottles being possibly no more than commercial containers of the Rhenish wine. However that may be, the importation was sufficiently large to suggest the thought of a native stoneware manufacture. In the reign of Queen Elizabeth I, a certain William Simpson, in petitioning for a monopoly to import the German wares, undertook to "draur to the making of such like pottes into some decayed town within the realm, wherebie manie a hundred poor men may be sett at work". It is not known, however, what became of this project, and no certainly English stoneware pot of this period has been identified.

B

STUART

Lead-glazed earthenware. Lead-glazed earthenware has had a continuous history in England from at least Anglo-Saxon, and probably from Roman, times. We have seen what improvements the characteristic medieval forms of this pottery underwent in the Tudor period: in the seventeenth century, however, it takes on a special character. Whereas in the sixteenth century the potters had had recourse, in much of their best work, to a glaze coloured green with copper and to decoration formed by moulding, in the seventeenth century other forms of ornamentation come to the fore. The first hints of these developments are to be seen in the sixteenth century, when, particularly in some of the northern potteries, a dark-bodied earthenware was decorated by means of pads of white clay cut into designs and applied to the vessel (see p. 13, Pls. 3C, E). This technique was taken up and greatly developed during the succeeding century. The earliest large and coherent body of wares decorated by this means, however, is to be credited to one of the southern counties. At Wrotham, in Kent, a brickworks was already at work towards the end of the sixteenth century, and on the site a number of wasters have been found of the hard-fired red pottery with a dark glaze which, if of sixteenth-century date, would be called "Cistercian" ware (see p. 13). Pottery of this character was still made in the seventeenth century, however, and the Wrotham wasters are, no doubt, those of the common everyday pots made for purely utilitarian purposes (cf., however, Pl. 6A). Of far greater interest is the large series of pieces decorated with white "slip" (clay of a creamy consistency) which can be associated with the Wrotham potters. The earliest of these are usually more elaborate versions of the Tudor "tyg", already referred to (p. 13) – mugs with slightly outsplayed sides, with three or more handles disposed at equal intervals round the perimeter of the pot (Pl. 6B, cf. Pls. 3D, E, F). Such early pieces (the first dated example is of 1612) are usually sparingly ornamented with pads of white clay bearing simple impressed devices such as rosettes, plant-sprays, fleurs-de-lis, lions rampant and the like: the double-loop handles are frequently decorated with a twist of red-and-white clay let into the upper loop, which is surmounted by a white cottage-loaf finial (Pl. 6B). Towards the middle of the century the decoration becomes more elaborate, with liquid white slip being applied from a spouted can in dots and dashes, or forming simple decorative motifs and inscriptions. The dashes were frequently used in conjunction with the applied pads in such a way that the latter looked as if stitched on to the pot. The red clay used was of two tones – a darker showing deep-brown under the glaze, and a lighter showing up as reddish-brown – while the white slip appeared of a cream or yellowish tint owing to the iron impurities in the glaze. The pots were frequently stamped with initials (Pl. 6A), and these can in many cases be connected with potters known to be working in Wrotham at the time. The dated series continues until at least 1739.

It is evident that the elaborately decorated wares described were not ordinary productions, but must have been made especially for weddings, christenings, betrothals and the like. They often bear, in addition to the potter's initials, those of the intended recipient. In one case the initials are those of the potter and the girl whom he is known to have married. The forms most frequently found, apart from the "tyg" already described, are globular cups with a single handle of the double-looped form, elaborate four-nozzled candlesticks, jugs, puzzle-jugs and, very rarely, large dishes. These last are remarkable, not only for their rarity and large size, but also because they are decorated in an exceptional technique. The dish was first coated with a layer of "slip", and the design was then cut through this layer to the red clay below, showing up in red on cream (*sgraffiato* technique).

Far less ambitious and fanciful than the Wrotham wares, but overlapping them in date, is a kind of slipware which is frequently found in the London region and must have been made there. These wares, usually jugs, mugs (Pl. 7A) and cups, are decorated in a rather thin cream-coloured slip on a light red ground. The majority of dated examples fall in the second quarter of the seventeenth century, and this fact and the circumstance that many of them bear pious inscriptions (such as "Remember God" or "For Earth I am") suggest that this pottery was made either for Puritans or to conform with the canons of propriety expected in a predominantly Puritan city. The same considerations may have dictated the somewhat impoverished style of decoration which is common to most of them. This consists of little more than one or two feathery stylizations of acanthus leaves, groups of dashes, wavy lines and the like. The absence of later dated pieces has prompted the suggestion that the potteries which made this ware were destroyed in the Fire of London in 1666.

Of much greater consequence were the slipwares made in Staffordshire. Here, in due course, practically every possible combination of the potentialities of slip-decoration was triumphantly exploited. This whole class of slipwares has sometimes been called "Toft" ware, from a name which appears frequently on some of the finest examples of this pottery. These are normally large dishes, some 17 to 22 in. in diameter and 3 in. deep, with a flat base and a broad, flat rim (Pl. 8A). Such pieces are normally coated with a layer of white slip (showing up rather yellowish under the lead-glaze), and the design is then drawn on with a darkish brown slip, any areas required to be of a solid colour being filled in with a slip of a redder tone. The rim was decorated with a trellis pattern of contrasting lines of the two red slips. Finally, the design in the well of the dish was picked out with dots of a white slip, which endow it with a lively sparkle. The motifs most popular on these dishes include loyal portraits of Charles II and Catherine of Braganza, the royal and other arms, and emblems, such as the Pelican in her Piety and the Mermaid combing her hair. Signed Toft pieces are known dated 1671 and 1674, whilst a third piece may have been made before 1680. These great dishes were almost certainly not the routine productions of the potters who made them, but, like the Wrotham wares, commemorated special events in the lives of the people who commissioned them; and they would have stood on dressers for show, rather than have been exposed to risk in use. The same may be said of the large and elaborate many-handled posset-pots (cf. Pl. 8c) of a slightly later date, and of the model cradles, often of a considerable size, which were made to commemorate the birth of a child (Pl. 8b). To this circumstance we no doubt owe the survival of a surprisingly large number of these fine pieces.

To the technical repertory of the potters of the great slipware dishes (Pls. 8a, 9a), the latter part of the seventeenth century made a number of additions. Notable among these was the use of slip-combing, in which trails of slip, contrasting in colour with the surface of the piece to be decorated, were laid on in parallel lines and then "combed" into feather patterns by drawing a point across the lines so made (Pl. 7b). Slightly dished oblong trays with patterns produced in this way have continued to be made in country potteries from that day to this.

Another way of handling slip-trailing was to lay on the lines of contrasting slip and then, by jogging the dish, to cause them to run into patterns somewhat resembling those of marbled papers. The Staffordshire (and other) potters also availed themselves of the *sgraffiato* technique already referred to, which also exploits the contrasting colours of dark and light clays. Finally, the second half of the seventeenth century saw the introduction of a method of decoration which was fraught with significance for the future development of the pottery industry in Staffordshire. This was the use of convex moulds of hard-baked clay, into which designs had been incised while it was still soft. Over these were pressed thick sheets of clay, the design being thereby transferred in raised outline. Into the depressions so formed, clay of contrasting colours could be poured to obtain the necessary chromatic effects. This technique was the first portent of the mass-production methods which were, in the eighteenth century, to make the pottery industry one of the leaders in the Industrial Revolution (see p. 38).

Staffordshire, however, although coming in the course of the seventeenth century to a prominence which it never subsequently lost, was only one of many centres in which lead-glazed pottery was made. Dark-glazed pottery had been made in Derbyshire in the previous century, and Tickenhall in particular is credited with a type of ware in which designs were cut out from pads of white clay and applied on a dark ground (see p. 13): less plausible is the attribution to this centre of a number of the types of slipware already here ascribed to Stafford-shire. It seems reasonable, however, to credit the Derbyshire potteries with some of the particularly hard pottery with dark, almost metallic, glaze which seems to carry on the Tickenhall characteristics of the sixteenth century in shapes of the seventeenth century, or even later. Somewhat similar pottery, with dark-brown glaze shading off into various tones of purple and green, was made at a variety of centres in the Stuart period. In Wiltshire, somewhere in the vicinity of Salisbury, a red-bodied pottery, usually with a dark purplish-brown glaze, was decorated by means of incised or applied inscriptions (Pl. 8c), sprays of foliage, interlaced ornaments and so forth. Somewhat similar wares were made at Buckland, in Buckinghamshire, from 1701 onwards. At Gestingthorpe, in Essex, in the course of the eighteenth century, was made an analogous red-bodied pottery, covered with a yellow glaze flecked with dark brown, and decorated with incised inscrip-tions and rough sprays of flowers: since there was a brick-works here in 1693, it is reasonable to infer that pottery of this type was made in the period under review also.

All the pottery so far described owes its decoration solely to the use of various coloured clays under the yellowish lead-glaze of the period, or to incised orna-ments. At other centres, however, advantage was taken of the possibilities of staining the glaze itself by means of copper- or manganese-oxide. At Donyatt, in Somersetshire, were made "tygs", posset-pots, dishes and other shapes, decorated by scratching through a white slip to the red clay, and by staining the otherwise yellow glaze with a green mottling produced by means of brass or copper filings. Many of these pieces bear dates in the second half of the seventeenth century. To Fareham, in Hampshire, is ascribed a type of posset-pot made of a light-red clay and decorated with simple designs and inscriptions formed from notched strips of light-coloured clay, often stained purple or green with manganese or copper. These mostly bear dates in the opening years of the eighteenth century.

Stoneware. Stoneware is a type of pottery made of a clay sufficiently resistant to withstand firing at very high temperatures – so high that the clay vitrifies. Such a substance is in itself impervious to liquids. To improve its appearance, however, a glaze was often used on it. This was obtained by shovelling into the kiln, at the height of the firing, quantities of common salt. This volatilised, and combined with the constituents of the clay to form a glassy surface-layer on it.

It was observed in the last chapter that stoneware had been imported into England from Germany in quantity during the sixteenth century, and that in Queen Elizabeth I's reign there was an attempt to replace this costly import by a home-manufacture. Nothing is known of the fate of that venture. The same tale is repeated in the seventeenth century. In 1626 a patent was granted to Thomas Rous and Abraham Cullen to "use, exercise, practise, and put in use the arte and feate of frameing, workeing, and makeing of all and all manner of potte, jugge, and bottelle, commonly called or knowne by the name or names of stone potte, stone jugge, and stone bottelle. ..." Nothing is known of the stoneware, if any, made by this partnership, and the same is true of another joint patent granted in 1635 to three capitalists seeking to exploit the coal-firing process for, among other things, the "Makeinge and Dyeinge of all sortes of Panne Tyles, Stone Juggs, Bottles of all sizes ... and other Earthen Comodityes within this our Realme, which nowe are made by Straungers in Forraigne Partes; ..."

The commonest form of stoneware, as these quotations show, was the wine-bottle or -pot, the former, like those which we came across in our survey of the Tudor period, most frequently being decorated with a bearded head in applied moulded relief (Pl. 10B), and usually referred to as "Bellarmines" after the hated Cardinal of that name (see p. 17). The bottles are supposed to satirize the Cardinal's short stature, his full figure and his hard countenance.

At a later date, however, as has been pointed out by Mr Martin Holmes,[1] "the man with the beard" came to be identified with the great Duke of Alva, another anti-Reformation personality well hated in northern Europe. Evelyn the diarist wrote in 1697 of Alva: "Of whom there are a Thousand Pictures (not on medals only, but on every Jugg-Pot & Tobacco Box) showing a most malicious, stern and merciless aspect, fringed with a prolix and squalid Beard, which draws down his meager and hollow Cheeks, Emblems of his Disposition." Whoever was represented, the "jug faced with a beard" was a commonplace of seventeenth-century literature: and the innumerable fragments of such bottles which are excavated in this country bear witness to their almost universal employment. Most of them were probably made in the Rhineland, although some may be the unrecognized products of the kilns of Rous and Cullen. When we come to the second half of the seventeenth century, however, we are on safer ground.

In 1671 a patent was granted to a certain John Dwight for "the Mistery of Transparent Earthenware, Comonly knowne by the Names of Porcelain or China, and Persian Ware, as alsoe the Misterie of the Stone Ware, vulgarly called Cologne Ware". In 1676, and again in 1677, John Dwight entered into contracts with the Company of Glass Sellers to supply them with stonewares. On the site of Dwight's pottery at Fulham were discovered in the nineteenth century a certain number of stoneware bottles which must have been of his making (Pl. 10B). They reveal certain differences from the normal German stonewares, to be seen in the details of the medallions applied to the body of the bottles, and in the technical peculiarity that they do not appear to have been cut from the wheel with a string, therefore do not show the elliptical string-marks on the base which are a common feature of German stoneware pots. Dwight's fine stonewares, however, were of quite a different order. Dwight himself had been an ecclesiastical lawyer, and was a characteristic man of the late seventeenth century – many-sided, interested

[1] Martin Holmes, "The So-Called 'Bellarmine' Mask on Imported Rhenish Stoneware", *Antiquaries' Journal* XXXI (1951), pp. 173 ff.

in the arts and sciences, and, above all, of an experimental frame of mind, like a true member of the Royal Society. As the terms of his patent show, he imagined himself to have discovered the secret of making porcelain. It is evident, however, from his recipes, some of which have come down to us in transcripts from his own notebooks, that what he made was a whitish salt-glazed stoneware, often so thinly

A Decantor

A Carved Teapot

A Flower-Pot

A Mogg

A Carved Jug

A Capuchine

Such as have Occation for these Sorts of Pots commonly called Stone-Ware, or for Such as are of any other Shape not here Represented may be furnished w.th them by the Maker James Morley at y Pot-House ʒ Nottingham

Fig. 1. Copperplate advertisement of the Nottingham stoneware potter, James Morley, about 1700. *The Bodleian Library, Oxford.*

potted as to be translucent. The drab, mouse-coloured and brown colours at his disposal were skilfully exploited by Dwight to produce a variety of decorative effects. White and mouse-coloured clays were kneaded together to produce a marbled effect; white reliefs were used on a brown ground; and occasionally oxide of cobalt was employed to stain a white clay blue. By these means were produced bottles and mugs of a very high ceramic quality. Far more important, however, were the figures made in the same materials. These are usually regarded, and rightly so, as representing a zenith in English pottery. Not only did the material lend itself admirably to modelling, its tightly-fitting glaze in no way obscuring sharpness of detail, but the figures were made by an artist of great skill. It is not known who he was, but it may have been Dwight himself; his fellow-member of the Royal Society, Dr Plot, said of him that he had "so far advanced the *Art Plastick* that 'tis dubious whether any Man since Prometheus have excelled *him*, not excepting the famous *Damophilus* and *Gorgasus* of *Pliny*." The Dwight figures include Royal portraits and mythological personages, but the most eloquent of all are undoubtedly the effigies of the potter's own daughter, Lydia, one showing the child recumbent on her death-bed, the other showing her rising in her shroud to meet the Resurrection (Pl. 11A). They reveal a very strong feeling in the artist.

In 1693–94 John Dwight brought actions against a number of other potters for infringing his patent of 1684, which confirmed and extended the patent of 1671. Among those named were Aaron, Thomas and Richard Wedgwood, of Burslem, in Staffordshire, and James Morley, of Nottingham. Little is known of stoneware-potting in Staffordshire at this date, but it is an interesting fact that in a list of Staffordshire potters working about 1710, drawn up to Josiah Wedgwood considerably later in the century, Dr Thomas Wedgwood is shown as making "brown stone", whilst others made "stone" and "freckled" ware. These literary references are supported both by fragments of stoneware excavated in Staffordshire and by intact pieces of almost certain Staffordshire origin. Of the former class are fragments of mugs decorated with bands of horizontal reeding and applied relief-sprigging of characteristic seventeenth-century type: some of them bear the crowned cypher AR, and come from mugs of certified capacity. Although these initials are not always to be taken at their face-value, in this case there is no reason to think that the mugs were not made in the reign of Queen Anne. Furthermore, in the Enoch Wood Collection (assembled in Staffordshire in the early nineteenth century, before the trade in antiquities had properly begun) were three small mugs which are relevant in this context. One is in buff stoneware with a broad brown band round the top: the other two are of virtually identical shape, but of a mottled lead-glazed earthenware. It is reasonable to assume that the first is of the "dipped white stoneware" referred to by Wedgwood, while the others are of the "freckled" ware. Either category, but especially the first, might be classed as the "brown mugs" of Dwight's law-suit.

The case of James Morley is simpler. Stonewares of a lustrous light-brown surface are known with inscriptions which connect them with Nottingham, and with dates commencing in 1700. These pieces, often decorated with incised designs or with ornaments pierced through the outer layer of a double-wall (Pl. 11C), frequently agree in shape and style with those represented in Morley's own trade-card, now preserved in the Bodleian Library, Oxford (Fig. 1).

Of greater ultimate importance than either the Wedgwoods or James Morley, however, were two other potters indicted at the same time in Dwight's suit. These were John and David Elers, then of Fulham, who were accused of infringing the patent as regards "brown muggs and red theapotts", corresponding to the "Cologne" wares and the "Opaceous, Redd, and Dark coloured Porcellane or China and Persian Wares ..." of Dwight's patent. These red teapots imitated the stoneware teapots of Yi-hsing, which were at this time being imported into England by the East India Company (see p. 29 below). Probably as a result of Dwight's litigation, the Elers withdrew to Staffordshire, and set up a pottery at Bradwell Wood, near Newcastle-under-Lyme. The scientist Martin Lister wrote in the *Philosophical Transactions* for 1693: "I have this to add, that this clay, *Haematites*, is as good, if not better than that which is brought from the *East Indies*. Witness the *teapots* now to be sold at the potters in the *Poultry* in *Cheapside*, which not only for art, but for beautiful color too, are far beyond any we have from *China*; these are made from the *English Haematites* in Staffordshire, as I take it, by two Dutchmen, incomparable artists." The work of the Elers has been reasonably well determined. It consists of unglazed red teapots, globular mugs (Fig. 2), reeded straight-sided mugs, cups and saucers, and tea-bottles (small caddies). Most of these pieces are decorated with sprays of flowers and leaves moulded in relief, but some have figural decorations in relief on recessed panels, the latter being, in one instance, backed with gilding. One or two examples of the Elers' work are known which are decorated with simple enamelling. This is perhaps the first enamelling carried out on European ceramics, and is noteworthy for this reason, if for no other. The Elers were apparently silversmiths by training, and the transference from metal-work to pottery of a technique hitherto exclusive to the former may well have occurred more readily to them than to more ordinary potters. This jewel-like enamelling (Pl. 11B), mainly in white, may well have a continuous history in England from the Elers' time down to the middle of the eighteenth century. A dated example of 1706 shows that it survived the Elers' period of activity in Staffordshire, for they are known to have returned to London by 1700 at the latest. Their importance resides in the fact that by the fineness of their work they set a standard hitherto undreamed of in Staffordshire. It was destined to inspire the potters there during the vital formative period of the industry in the first half of the eighteenth century.

Tin-glazed earthenware ("delftware"). The expression "delftware" is something of a misnomer in so far as the greater part of the tin-glazed pottery made in England during the seventeenth century is concerned, for the industry was well established in this country long before Delft rose to eminence as a city of potters. In fact, the making of tin-glazed earthenware, as was shown in the last chapter, was transplanted here from the Spanish Netherlands. They had, in turn, received it from Italy, the fountain-head of this painted pottery (there called *maiolica*). English "delftware" potteries are known in the late sixteenth century both in East Anglia and in Aldgate, London. Although some "delftware" was made in

Norwich during the second half of the seventeenth century, however, the emphasis throughout the Stuart period is on London. Here, apart from the Aldgate pottery already mentioned, two factories existed in Southwark in the first half of the seventeenth century – in the parishes of St Olave's and St Saviour's. To the certainly English pottery of the period 1600–60 it is, therefore, more accurate to give the label "Southwark" or "London", rather than the more usual "Lambeth"; since it was not until the period 1660–80 that one or more potteries making "gallyware" (as it was called by contemporaries) began operations at Lambeth. The position is complicated by the fact that potters from Southwark migrated about the middle of the century to Brislington, near Bristol, and founded a pottery there: this, in turn, hived off a factory in Bristol itself (the Temple pottery) in 1683. In evidence given before a Committee of the House of Commons in 1698 it was stated that "there are 7 White Earthen-warehouses about *London*: Two at *Bristoll*; and One at *Norwich*, which is since broke". To the potteries of the London area already mentioned should be added at least one, and probably two, at Vauxhall; while towards the end of the Stuart period (in 1710) the manufacture of "delftware" was begun in Liverpool.

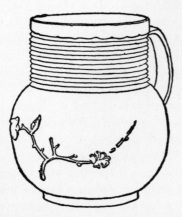

Fig. 2. Unglazed red stoneware mug with relief decoration, mounted with a silver band round the lip. Staffordshire (Bradwell Wood, factory of the brothers Elers), c. 1700.

Tin-glazed pottery is a lightly-fired earthenware covered with a lead-glaze made an opaque-white by the use of oxide (ashes) of tin. Its virtues reside in the beauty of the dense white glaze itself, and in the possibilities which it opens up of decoration by painting. Painting on ware of this type, however, offers its own special difficulties. The pottery is first fired to a porous "biscuit" condition, in which state it readily soaks up the glaze mixture (ground glaze suspended in water) into which it is dipped. On this somewhat rough base the painter has to carry out his designs without benefit of rubbings-out or *pentimenti*. These exacting conditions demand of the practitioner sureness of touch, and the chief virtues of delftware-painting are directness and boldness. The pigments used have to be such that they stand up to a considerable degree of heat in the second firing, when glaze and painting are developed together by the fire. The range of these metallic pigments is therefore limited, being restricted in practice to cobalt-oxide for blue, manganese-oxide for purple and brown tones, copper-oxide for green, antimony for yellow and iron for red.

The "delftwares" made at the beginning of the Stuart period were probably mostly in the general style of the contemporary Netherlands wares, with their echoes of Italian *maiolica*, being painted in the blue, purple, green, yellow and orange palette favoured at the time. Very little pottery of any pretension survives from the first two decades of the seventeenth century, however, and it is not until the founding of the Southwark potteries that an individual English style develops. At first it is most apparent in the shapes used. Typical among these is a small barrel-shaped mug (Pl. 13A), and although of these one of the earliest (1628) is decorated with no more than an overall speckling in manganese-purple, while a later example (1642) still displays the polychrome ornamentation of grotesques derived from the *maiolica* of Urbino, a small number of such mugs, of dates about 1630, are decorated in an entirely new way. Between borders of lines or conventional ornament are painted figures of birds standing on rocks amidst flowers and foliage, with an occasional insect flying in the interspaces (Pl. 13A). Both border-patterns and bird motifs are clearly copied from the imported Chinese porcelain of the Wan Li period (1573–1619),[1] but they are painted with a naïve charm of their own. One finds similarly decorated straight-sided mugs, spouted covered posset-pots, and wine-bottles of the same general shape as Dwight's stonewares (p. 24 above). As important as the decoration is the Chinese-inspired palette in which it is carried out – soft blue on the (sometimes pinkish) white of the glaze. This cool colour-scheme was extended to the embellishment of a range of wares which owed nothing else to imported porcelain – plates, posset-pots, porringers, candlesticks and wine-bottles decorated with nothing more than a coat-of-arms or a cartouche containing the owner's initials and a date; or, in the case of the wine-bottles, little more than the name of the wine, the date and a calligraphic scroll below them in the manner of the flourished signatures of the period (Pl. 13B). This beautiful pottery was made from the 1630's until the 1680's. The dense white glaze which constitutes its chief charm was occasionally left to speak for itself on pieces entirely undecorated by painting.

The "delftwares" so far described were all made for use. Contemporaneously, however, the London potters were turning out ambitiously painted dishes which were solely for decoration, to be displayed on the court-cupboards where richer people would range their plate. These pieces preserve the polychrome palette of an earlier period, and, from the circumstances that the great majority of them have a border of slanting blue brush-strokes, are familiarly known as "blue-dash chargers". The subjects chosen to decorate the centres of these showy pieces included biblical scenes, fruits and flowers, ships, coats-of-arms and representations of the Kings of England. Four types in particular were constantly repeated, and these form the most characteristic "Lambeth" and "Bristol" polychrome "delftwares" of the second half of the seventeenth century. These four are the chargers painted with the story of the Fall (Pl. 10A), with a spray of tulips and other

[1] See p. 31 below.

flowers (Pl. 10c), with representations of the reigning monarch (whether mounted, standing or half-length), or with vigorous formal designs of scrolls and curved strokes.

Apart from the decorative and functional pieces already described, mention should be made of the numerous vessels made for medical use. These consist mainly of spouted jars on pedestal feet, and of cylindrical pots, used to contain respectively liquid and dry medicaments; smaller pots for ointment, heart-shaped slabs elaborately painted with the arms of the Apothecaries' Company, for rolling pills, or merely for display; and, finally, one-handled bleeding bowls, and shaving-dishes with a segment out of the rim, illustrating the two aspects of the barber-surgeon's profession. These mainly utilitarian objects were normally decorated in blue only.

The blue-and-white colour-scheme continued in favour throughout the seventeenth and eighteenth centuries, especially in forms of decoration which were of oriental character (Pl. 9c); but towards the end of the seventeenth century the polychrome palette of the "blue-dash" chargers was discarded in favour of rather more sober schemes, in which blue, manganese-purple, red and green played a dominant part (Pl. 9b).

Oriental porcelain. Porcelain had reached England in only very small quantities during the sixteenth century, and was accordingly treated with the greatest respect, as its evident superiority to any European pottery warranted (see p. 15). In the inventory of Lettice, Countess of Leicester, "prized the viith day of January, 1634" was "Item, one pursland boule, with a guilt footte and a guilt cover. xlvs." (a considerable sum in those days). This may have been a treasured possession from an earlier period, for in the same inventory occurs the more casual entry "Item, six pursland fruit dishes": but the practice of mounting porcelain still continued at this time, as is shown by Pl. 12c – indeed, many pieces of this type were especially manufactured in China for mounting in Europe, the lid being made separately.

The most usual imports of porcelain during this early period were of bowls, dishes and vases (although smaller items were already being made to suit European taste – in 1638 Lady Brilliana Harley made a present to a friend of "two cruets of chinna, with silver and gilt covers, and bars and feete ..."). Thus, when some East India commodities were "put to sale by the candle for readie money" in London in 1618, the porcelain consisted of three "great deepe bason(s)"; and when the Dutch wished to make a present to Charles I in 1635, they selected "two large basins of China earth". This emphasis tended to shift somewhat with the introduction of the oriental beverages – tea and coffee – into England, and in Holland the Directors of the Dutch East India Company could write to their factors in Batavia in 1637: "As tea begins to come into use by some of the people, we expect some jars of Chinese as well as Japanese tea with every ship"; but the

earliest printed reference to tea in England seems to be a well-known advertisement in the *Commonwealth Mercury* of September, 1658. Of coffee, Evelyn wrote in
his *Memoirs* for 1637: "There came in my tyme to the Coll: one Nathaniel Cono-
pios out of Greece. ... He was the first I ever saw drink coffee, wh[ch] custom came
not into England till 30 years after." In this Evelyn was ten years or so out, for
from about 1652 that drink ("black as soote, and tasting not much unlike it", as
an earlier writer had said) was to be had of Pasqua Rosee in St Michael's Alley
in Cornhill. For exotic drinks, exotic cups were fitting; and from about the middle
of the century wares for the tea-table assume a greater importance. In 1637 the
Dutch East India Company ordered 25,000 tea-cups from its factors, and from
that date tea-wares formed a constant and important item in their porcelain re-
quisitions. This change of emphasis is paralleled in England. At a supper-party
given by Lady Gerrard in 1652 there is mention of cups and saucers of porcelain,
as well as of plates, all in considerable quantities. The saucer, from being a little
plate for sauce, as its name implies, was now to become the inseparable adjunct
of the tea-cup. Tea was extremely expensive at this period, costing anything between 25s. and three guineas per pound, and it was in consequence, no doubt,
drunk weak in the Chinese manner, and in small quantities.

Most of the porcelain so far described would have been of the blue-and-white
ware made at the great pottery-centre of Ching-tê Chên, in the Kiangsi province
of China. For the brewing of tea, however, "porcelain" of another sort was deemed
appropriate. This was the unglazed red stoneware of Yi-hsing, in Kiangsu, which
was highly esteemed by the Chinese themselves for the purpose: in Europe it was
sometimes, through confusion with a superficially similar Spanish ware, called
boccaro. Thus, in 1681 a Treasury Warrant issued to the Customs Commissioners
to permit the landing of "some pictures, pourcellin and Boucaros". The small teapots made from this red ware were usually decorated with sprays of prunus-
blossom in relief (Pl. 13c), and it is to such ware that an advertisement in the
London Gazette of 14th to 18th February 1695, refers: "At the Marine Coffee House
in Birchin-lane Cornhill, on Friday the 1st of March at 3 after Noon will be exposed to Sale by the Candle, fine red figured and flowered Tea Pots, Chocolate
Cups, and other Curiosities. ..." The red teapots, chocolate-cups, saucers and
tea-bottles were copied by the potters in Holland, and in England by John Dwight
and the Elers brothers (see p. 25 above).

The porcelain hitherto described has been mainly of a utilitarian character,
however exalted the uses to which it was put. At the same time, however, porcelain
vases and bowls were being used for purely decorative purposes, as one may
occasionally see them represented in the contemporary Dutch paintings of inter-
iors. Wycherley in his *Plain Dealer* (1674) makes Olivia say of porcelain that it is
"the most innocent and pretty furniture for a lady's chamber". Hitherto most of
the porcelain which had reached England had come via Holland. About this time,
however, it began to be imported by the English East India Company, although

considerable imports direct from China do not seem to have begun much before 1700. As to the scale of the trade at this date we have not only the records of the East India Company, but the words of a contemporary seaman, a certain Barlow, who was serving as chief mate and China pilot on the *Fleet Frigate*: "... And having all things ready, on Monday the 1st day of February 1702–3, we set sail from a place called 'Whampow' in the river of Canton in China, praying God for a good passage to England, being a full ship and laden with goods, namely: 205 chests of China and Japan ware, porcelain... and a great deal more loose China and Japan earthenware, which was packed up on board...." The great quantities, often running into tens of thousands of pieces, which suddenly flooded the market as the East Indiamen reached home, caused the prices of porcelain to fluctuate violently. Thus it stands on record that in 1699 "the price of chinaware is fallen 12s. in the pound". Normally, however, the demand for porcelain was greater than the supply, and in years of war prices might rise to three times the normal. In addition to the inherent high cost of a rare commodity brought from so far away, the English customer had to pay duty on his porcelain at the rate of 33 per cent.

Despite high prices, however, enormous quantities of porcelain were absorbed by Europe during the second half, and particularly the last quarter, of the seventeenth century; and it began to be used purely for decoration in a way hitherto undreamed of. This fashion was given in England the supreme impetus of being taken up by the Queen. Already whilst still in Holland, Queen Mary had contracted a passion for porcelain, and in her country residence of Hunsslardiek, near The Hague, she had an audience chamber which was described in 1687 as "very richly furnished with Chinese work and pictures ... The chimney-piece was full of precious porcelain, part standing half inside it, and so fitted together that one piece supported another." This interior must have been the modest counterpart of certain rooms in German palaces, where every available space was filled with great pyramids of porcelain of every shape and size. This conception, on a more modest scale, was carried to England when King William III and his Queen began to rebuild and redecorate Hampton Court in 1689. The traces of this provision for porcelain are still to be seen in the shelf-topped corner fireplaces in many of the rooms, and much of Queen Mary's Chinese and Japanese porcelain is still to be found there (Pls. 12A, B). Defoe wrote in his *Tour thro' the Whole Island of Great Britain* (1724–27): "The Queen brought in the Custom or Humour, as I may call it, of furnishing Houses with *China*-Ware, which increased to a strange degree afterwards, piling their *China* upon the tops of Cabinets, scrutores, and every Chimney-piece, to the Tops of the Ceilings, and even setting up Shelves for their *China*-ware, where they wanted such Places. ..." This was indeed the China-mania, of which we hear already in Wycherley's *The Country Wife* (first acted 1672 or 1673), when Lady Fidget says: "What, d'ye think if he had had any left, I would not have had it too? for we women of quality never think we have china enough."

As has already been said, the vast majority of the pieces brought home from

China were blue-and-white, and these display the changing styles of the time, from the Wan-li (1573–1619) plates and dishes, with their birds on rocks, deer and other motifs, through the "Transitional" period (Pl. 12A) consequent upon the breakdown of Ming power, to the classic period of K'ang Hsi (1662–1722), when the power of the Manchu dynasty was stabilized upon the Imperial Throne. Occasional pieces in other modes of decoration, however, reached Europe. Queen Mary possessed late-Ming wares with purple-and green-dappled glazes, and the East India Company records make reference to other types of coloured wares. Japanese porcelain, particularly that from Arita, exported by the Dutch through their trading centre near Nagasaki, was much favoured; and at Hampton Court are some splendid pieces in the Kakiemon style from Queen Mary's collection (Pl. 12B). Side by side with such pieces in decorative *ensembles* might be found figures and vessels in the creamy *blanc-de-chine* porcelain made at Tê-hua, in Fukien (Pl. 12D).

EARLY GEORGIAN

Delftware. As we saw in the preceding chapters, the making of tin-glazed earthenware was practised in England already in the sixteenth century, and by the second half of the seventeenth century there were a number of factories at work, both in the London area and in Bristol and the neighbouring Brislington. During the eighteenth century new factories sprang up (notably in Liverpool, where by about 1760 a dozen or so were active), whilst a few of the older-established works were forced to close down. Some of the latter have already been referred to in our survey of the Stuart period (see p. 26). In the London area there were manufactures near the Hermitage Dock, Wapping (until at least 1724); at Southwark, where one pottery in the parish of St Olave's and St John's continued working until late in the eighteenth century, whilst a second, in the parish of St Saviour's, appears to have closed down before the middle of the century; at Lambeth, where two factories were at work for the greater part of the period under review; and at Vauxhall. The Brislington pottery had disappeared by 1750, but there were three factories at work in Bristol itself – the Temple pottery, St Mary Redcliffe's and Limekiln Lane, of which the last-named had ceased production in 1754. Delftware was also manufactured at Wincanton, in Somerset (Pl. 15A). Apart from the English potteries, there were more or less short-lived enterprises in Glasgow, Dublin and Limerick.

The late seventeenth century had seen the supercession of earlier types of delftware by pottery almost exclusively inspired by Chinese porcelain, of which very large quantities were imported at the time. Apart from the blue-and-white colourscheme, which, from the second quarter of the century, had symbolized the ascendancy of oriental wares, a bright polychromy of red, blue, green and yellow mimicked the enamelled wares of the late Ming and K'ang Hsi (1662–1722) periods. In this palette were painted not only more or less direct copies of Chinese designs and more fanciful *chinoiseries*, but boldly brushed-in patterns of purely European inspiration, such as a windmill, a fish (Fig. 3), a swan swimming or a cock in a landscape. In the eighteenth century, as in the seventeenth, delftware was a useful outlet for the expression of political sentiment (Pl. 18A). Towards 1750 a gradual change comes over the colours used by the English delftware painters;

they grow paler and softer, and in general conform to the changed colour-sense characteristic of the rococo, as opposed to the baroque, movement in art. About the same time, a form of plate characterized by a low foot-rim, taken over from imported Chinese porcelain, was universally adopted (Pls. 15A, B; Fig. 4). This plate is the commonest of all forms in delftware during the period we are considering, but the first half of the century saw the evolution of many shapes unknown in the seventeenth century, catering for most domestic needs. For drinkers of strong

Fig. 3. Plate of blue-painted delftware, Bristol, c. 1730.

drinks there were punch-bowls (Pl. 14B), tankards (sometimes with glass bases), monteiths, wine-labels and puzzle-jugs (Pl. 15C). For tea-drinkers, despite the unsuitable nature of the material, which did not stand up well to sudden changes of temperature, there were tea-cups and saucers, tea-pots, sugar-bowls, cream-jugs and tea-trays (Pl. 14A); for those who favoured coffee, coffee-cups and pots. For the service of the dinner-table, apart from the plates and dishes, there were sauce-boats, tureens, and even gravy-argyles; and in apartments other than the dining-room there were bowls with perforated tops to hold flowers; rectangular "bricks" similarly pierced for the same purpose, or in some instances adapted as inkstands, with a central large hole for the ink-well; and candlesticks copied from silver models. For the sick-room or nursery there was the food-warmer, in which the food

Fig. 4. Cross-section of plate common to the English delftware factories from c. 1725–30 onwards.

c

was kept hot by a small lamp, the cover being fitted with a candle-holder (Pl. 15D); whilst in the bedrooms the exiguous toilet of the eighteenth century was catered for by a small basin and a waterbottle the size of a modern carafe.

The bold, simple forms of decoration of the early eighteenth century gave way during its second quarter to a softer and more elegant style better attuned to the changing taste of the period. Ladies and gentlemen in contemporary costume stroll through European landscapes (Pl. 15C), and delicate *chinoiserie* scenes evoke some of the qualities of space and atmosphere which are characteristic of true Chinese painting, and which in England may look forward, as one authority has pointed out, to the achievements of the English School of water-colourists (Pl. 14B). On a different plane were the many designs, painted with far less sophistication, which reproduced naïve *chinoiseries*, versions of Chinese porcelain bird- and flower-painting (see p. 27), or simply rather artless European subjects of figures or flowers (Pls. 15A, B, D).

The English delftware potters of the eighteenth century were responsible for a number of innovations, not all of which were entirely original. The powdered grounds of Chinese porcelain were copied in cobalt-blue and manganese-purple (Pl. 15A), whilst a sponge charged with colour was often used to dab in the foliage of trees. One technique which in the eighteenth century was almost exclusive to England was the use, on a glaze tinged bluish or greenish, of designs drawn in opaque-white (*bianco-sopra-bianco*), a method of decoration which had its technical roots in the Italian *maiolica* of the Renaissance, but which may have owed its immediate inspiration to the incised designs on some Chinese porcelain (Pl. 15B). The use of over-glaze enamelling and gilding on a tin-glaze, so widely familiar in the contemporary faïence of the Continent, is extremely rare in England, and is found only on some Liverpool delftware. Uncommon too, although characteristically English, was the employment of transfer-printing, found occasionally on Liverpool (and Irish) pieces.

Lead-glazed earthenware. English lead-glazed pottery of the early Georgian period is characterized by a striving after refinement. Although in many parts of the country "slipwares" of the types described in the previous chapter continued to be made, their use was confined to the humbler orders of society. Meanwhile, in North Staffordshire, where the most interesting slipwares of the seventeenth century had been made, great changes were afoot. Although pieces made in the old techniques certainly survived into the period under discussion, even they reveal in many instances an elegance not distinguishable in the earlier wares (Pl. 16B). This tendency can be traced to two causes – the growing awareness of the qualities of imported Chinese porcelain (with which was included the unglazed red stoneware of Yi-hsing), and the memory of the Elers brothers, whose important contribution to the pottery of their own period has already been described (see p. 25). The fine quality and finish of the work produced by the Elers brothers in imitation of Yi-hsing stoneware pottery must have made a most forcible impression on the contemporary Staffordshire makers, and borne in on them the realization that such things were possible for them too. The unglazed redwares continued to be made throughout the eighteenth century (Pl. 17A), but the trend away from the more primitive wares of the past is to be more clearly seen in other forms of pottery, and in other techniques.

Perhaps the earliest variant is a type of ware which still employs the brown-and-white colour-scheme of slipware, but which also uses the newer technique of decoration by means of reliefs stamped from pads of white clay and applied to the brown body of the piece (Pl. 17B, cf. Pls. 3C, E, 6B, 7). This type of relief-decorated pottery has traditionally been attributed to John Astbury (1686–1743), but it was certainly also made by Thomas Whieldon (1719–1795), at Fenton Low, and probably by other potters too. Astbury is also credited by tradition with two innovations which were of crucial importance at this stage of the industry. These were the use of Devonshire white clay as a surface-wash to darker clays; and the introduction of calcined flint into the body of wares, to make them whiter and lighter. The latter innovation is alternatively attributed to Thomas Heath, of Lane Delph, Staffs; but the whiteness of calcined flint was at this period familiar in the glass industry, and would naturally recommend itself as a possible ingredient to potters looking for materials in which to imitate the whiteness of porcelain. This practice seems to have been introduced during the 1720's, and although the use of calcined flint was more immediately appreciated in the manufacture of white salt-glazed stoneware (see p. 38 below), its use in earthenware bodies made possible the development of the coloured lead-glazes discussed below. The "Astbury–Whieldon" phase of the industry's development is perhaps best illustrated by the group of pieces shown in Pl. 18B. Here are the colour contrasts familiar from the earlier wares – the white of handle and spout against the warm brown or buff of the body – accompanied by one or two technical innovations. Instead of the stamped relief-decoration of the "Astbury" wares (cf. Pl. 17B), the ornament was obtained by "luting" to the surface of the pot previously moulded relief-motifs, and by connecting these with "stems" formed of threads of clay rolled out thin between the hands. This whole process was known as "sprigging". A pointer to things to come is the use of dabs of colour to enliven the leaves and flowers of the sprigged decoration. The use of metallic oxides to produce colours is familiar in England from medieval times, as we have already noted, but it here makes its first appearance in Staffordshire. Coloured decoration had to await a further technical improvement before it could be used to its greatest advantage. This improvement consisted in the substitution of liquid-glazing for the older method of dusting with a powdered sulphide of lead (galena). By the newer technique, the piece, fired once to the "biscuit" condition, was dipped into a mixture of powdered glaze and water, which it soaked up evenly. This smooth glaze, when laid on the improved white body, was a perfect medium for the development of decoration by means of colouring oxides. Yellow, green, purplish-brown, and particularly a slate blue and grey, were used in patches laid on without any particular pattern. At their best, particularly when the grey is used with one or two other colours, the pieces so decorated have a softness and charm peculiarly their own: sometimes, however, as when the yellow and green are used in an "egg-and-spinach" combination, the effects are far less pleasing. Perhaps the most charming of all pieces made in this style are the artless figures, or "image-toys", of the "Astbury–Whieldon" phase. These, although perhaps inspired ultimately by porcelain, are, with some exceptions, original in conception and execution. Such are the little figures of seated musicians, or of men and women on horseback (Pl. 16c), or the grotesque adaptation of the classical "*spinario*" taking a thorn out of his foot, entirely changed in character by the substitution of an enormous lolling head. On the earlier members of this family some details are picked out in clays of contrasting colours, in addition to the coloured glazes, and these form a bridge between the figures of the "Astbury–Whieldon" class, and those of the "Astbury" group, in which all the colour contrasts are obtained solely by the use of clays of different tones.

Other wares made by the potters of this period include a pottery with a dense black glaze, and "agate-ware". The former, often called "Jackfield" pottery (from the place of that name in Shropshire), was certainly also made in Staffordshire and at Newcastle. The pieces with a dense black glaze and relief decoration are probably to be attributed to Staffordshire, whereas the true Jackfield wares are usually smooth of surface, browner in colour, and decorated with unfired painting or gilding. They are usually later in date (third quarter of the eighteenth century), and there can be no doubt that the art of making this pottery was transplanted there from Staffordshire. "Agate-ware" was made by mixing together dark and light clays (and frequently also a white clay stained blue with cobalt), to produce a marbled effect. This material would tolerate a minimum of handling, and could not therefore be used in thrown shapes, teapots and the like being made by pressing the clay into two-part moulds (Pl. 17A). This "true" agate-ware was at a later date imitated by means of a marbled surface-wash imparted to a plain clay base.

The technical improvements so far described have all been in the direction of refining the materials of body and glaze. One further, and vital, innovation affected the formation of the pot itself. This was the introduction of the plaster-of-Paris mould (reputedly by Ralph Daniel, in 1740). The use of moulds as a speedy way of duplicating shapes or decoration had already been appreciated by the makers of the earlier slipwares(see p. 20). In this phase, as we saw in the preceding chapter, a convex mould with an incised design was prepared in clay and fired hard. On this a slab of red clay was pressed, producing a hollow dish with an outline pattern in relief. Into the cells so formed a white slip was poured, thus producing a design in white on a dark ground, with a minimum expenditure of time and skill. These dishes continued to be made until about the middle of the eighteenth century, but in the meantime the practice of moulding had been greatly extended. The plates with dappled glazes, for instance, often have borders moulded in the form of basket-work and the like (Pl. 19A): these were formed by pressing a slab of clay down on a plate-shaped mould which had this design on its upper surface and which was fixed to the head of the wheel. The plate was then "thrown" in the normal way, the back and foot being profiled as desired. The crowning innovation in this movement towards labour-saving, however, was the plaster mould. First a master-mould was prepared in alabaster or the like, in the exact semblance of the body of the finished pot. From it a cast was taken, and from the cast a clay "block" was pressed. This was fired to stoneware hardness, to become the working model, and from it the plaster moulds were pulled. These moulds were made up in two or more sections, the design being in negative on the inside of the sections. Into the composite mould so formed, the clay was poured as a thin slip. The water was absorbed by the porous plaster, leaving a thin film of clay adhering to the inside of the mould. When this skin was of the desired thickness and the clay was sufficiently dry, the mould was taken apart, leaving the pot ready for the next stages of manufacture, with the decoration sharply defined on its surface.

Although used to a far greater extent by the stoneware potters, this technique was also employed at the end of the period to produce relief-decorated hollow-wares with colour-glazes. Some of the best of these are amongst the earliest productions of Josiah Wedgwood when working on his own account. His famous "cauliflower" and "pineapple" wares (teapots and so forth made in those forms), with their strong green and yellow glazes, were produced by this technique.

Salt-glazed stoneware. When in 1693 John Dwight brought his famous lawsuit in protection of his patent rights (see p. 24), he sued (besides the Elers brothers) potters in London, Nottingham and Staffordshire. Stoneware continued to be made in the London area in the eighteenth century, not only at Dwight's Fulham factory after his death, but also at Southwark, Lambeth Marsh and Mortlake. Some white stoneware was undoubtedly made, presumably in styles more or less resembling those in vogue in Staffordshire (see p. 38 below), but the majority must have been brown wares of a more or less utilitarian character. The most ambitious of them were large mugs decorated with drinking- or hunting-scenes in relief (Pl. 20A), or smaller isolated motifs, such as a head of Queen Anne, trees, rosettes and the like, of a sort familiar from the Fulham stoneware of the previous century. These mugs were usually of a buff body, the upper half being coloured a rich brown by means of a ferruginous wash applied before the piece was fired. They were frequently made to order for a particular publican, whose name is then found incised in the clay of the body.

Of a similar brown colour was the stoneware made at Nottingham throughout the eighteenth century (see p. 24). This pottery, however, far surpassed that made in the London area by dint of its lustrous surface, the fineness of its potting, and the fresh style of decoration with which it was most often embellished. Apart from repetitive designs made by stamping or rouletting, this ornamentation often included flower-sprays and the like freely incised when the clay was soft (Pls. 20B, 11C). A rarer, but charming, technique of decoration was the use of a "resist", whereby a design was protected from the surface wash, and therefore stood out in a lighter tone on the warm brown ground. Reliefs were also used, but far more sparingly than in either London or Staffordshire, and a not particularly attractive application of shreds of clay, giving bands of ornament resembling "rough-cast" (particularly favoured on the joke jugs made in the form of a bear, where the shreds of clay simulated fur). A very similar stoneware was produced at Crich, in Derbyshire.

Of far greater consequence than any of the wares so far dealt with, however, was the stoneware made in Staffordshire. As we noted in the previous chapter, amongst the defendants in Dwight's lawsuit had been members of the Wedgwood family, and it is possibly to the son of one of them, "Dr" Thomas Wedgwood of Burslem, that were due the great improvements which took place in the manufacture of salt-glazed stoneware in the eighteenth century. The wares complained of by Dwight, as was suggested in the last chapter, were probably mugs of a buffish stoneware, the upper parts dipped in a brown wash, technically very like the Fulham mugs already described; and the earliest "white" Staffordshire stonewares were probably on more or less purified varieties of this buffish body. The use of imported West Country clay and calcined flint, however, affected the manufacture of salt-glazed stoneware no less than that of lead-glazed earthenware, many of the potters being in fact makers of both. Comparable in technique and quality with the "Astbury–Whieldon" pottery decorated by means of contrasting clay-colours (see p. 35 above and Pl. 18B) was a type of stoneware traditionally and plausibly associated with the younger "Dr" Thomas Wedgwood. This consisted of a drab-coloured body decorated with neat reliefs in contrasting white, the rusticated spout and "crabstock" handle being often also made in the same white clay. The white reliefs, which mingled wyverns and figures of Bacchus with delicate scroll-work in the general manner of the "Bérain" style, were sometimes also ephemerally gilt by an unfired process (Pl. 19B). Thomas Wedgwood died in 1737, and the style of these wares is consistent with this date. Possibly slightly later than these wares, but overlapping them chronologically, was the pure white stoneware made of the improved body incorporating white clay and calcined flint. The appearance, on some of the pieces made in this material, of reliefs commemorating the capture of Portobello in 1739 (Pl. 21D), suggests that it was perfected during the 1730's; although isolated examples are known with dates as early as 1720. The earliest of the mature white stonewares are, like the contemporary earthenwares of the "Astbury-Whieldon" phase, decorated by applied moulded reliefs and "sprigging" (sometimes gilt or picked out with blue). The greatest development, however, took place on the introduction of the techniques of moulding described above (pp. 36–7).

These were enthusiastically taken up by the stoneware-potters, perhaps because their process, involving no glaze-dipping, favoured the making of very thin-walled vessels. The earliest moulded pieces are "open" shapes made by pressing a sheet of clay into a metal or alabaster mould, and little pickle- and spoon-trays were made by this means with decoration of a beautiful sharpness of definition. Of much greater significance, however, was the adoption of slip-casting in plaster-of-Paris moulds (see above, p. 36, and below, p. 46). From about 1745 onwards the Stafford-shire potters poured out an unceas-ing stream of fine hollow-wares made in this way – teapots, coffee-pots, cups, sauce-boats, tureens, tea-caddies, basins and many more. These are usually remarkable, not only for their fineness, but also for the force and humour of the relief decorations. These were often by no means "correct" or in any known style, being frequently a curious hotch-potch of motifs drawn from different sources – *chin-oiseries*, European figures, tree- and plant-forms, shells, heraldic ani-mals and so forth, combined in a naïve but often effective way. This unconventionality often extended to the form of the vessel itself (Pl. 21A). The authors of this very English manner were the men who made the original blocks

Fig. 5. Bell in the form of a woman, salt-glazed stone-ware, Staffordshire, *c.* 1740. Ht 5¾ in.

from which the plaster moulds were ultimately taken. Prominent among them were members of the Wood family (see p. 48), notably Aaron Wood (1717–85), to whom have been attributed also the vigorous and amusing salt-glaze "Pew Groups", modelled in the round and representing a man and woman courting, a pair of musicians, etc. (and cf. Fig. 5). These far surpass in originality and power the numerous contemporary small figures made in two-part moulds and repre-senting the Chinese deity Shou Lao or such historical figures as Doctor Sacheverell and Maria Theresa. These figures are often embellished with touches of cobalt-blue, a pigment which is also used to enliven the small figures of cats moulded in brown-and-white "agate-ware" (see p. 36 above), and the group of so-called "scratch-blue" wares. These comprise mugs (Pl. 21B), loving-cups and jugs, with incised decoration into which the cobalt pigment was rubbed before firing. The wares of this class are frequently dated, the years ranging between 1748 and 1776. Their shapes differ from those of most of the types of salt-glazed stoneware hitherto described, and it is possible that they were made in separate factories. Much, however, remains to be learned about them. It is certain, for example, that Whieldon made "scratch-blue" wares, although no intact example has been certainly identified.

This mild flirtation with colour, however, was of little significance beside a style of polychrome ornamentation which was both incomparably more effective and far more widely practised. This consisted of painting the surface of the finished pot with enamel pigments which had to be subsequently fired in a "muffle" kiln. A simple and restricted form of enamelling was being carried out on "Elers" and other stoneware in the early years of the eighteenth century (see above p. 25), and it is possible that the process was exploited continuously in Staffordshire from then onwards. The course of its development in the second quarter of the eighteenth century is obscure, but in its mature manifestations Staffordshire enamel-painting is clearly recognizable. It is marked by a violent palette which included turquoise-blue and leaf-green, pink, purple, red and yellow. These clamorous colours were used to embellish scenes derived from Boucher, *chinoiseries*, flower-sprays with great pink roses, landscapes (Pl. 21A), topical motives (such as portraits of the Young Pretender) and so on. In these wares the ambitions of the Staffordshire potters to rival porcelain were at last realized, and it may well have been to a piece of enamelled salt-glazed stoneware that the poetaster referred when he wrote:

> To please the noble dame, the courtly Squire
> Produced a Tea Pot made in Staffordshire.
> So Venus looked, and with such longing eyes
> When Paris first produced the golden prize.
> 'Such works as this', she cries, 'can England do?
> It equals Dresden, and excels St Cloud.' [1]

Porcelain. We have seen that Chinese porcelain began to enter Europe in increasing quantities during the seventeenth century. Whereas Charles I had been content to acquire single pieces of it, Louis XIV, at the end of the century, had ordered a whole service, consisting of hundreds of (presumably matching) pieces. Before Louis' death, however, France already had two factories of her own, making "soft-paste" porcelain – that is, a porcelain made essentially of white clay compounded with ground glass, as opposed to the true "hard-paste" porcelain of oriental type, made of china-clay and china-stone fused at a far higher temperature. These French factories were Rouen (making porcelain from 1673 until probably 1696) and Saint-Cloud, which received its letters patent in 1702. Very little porcelain was made at Rouen, and until the foundation of the Meissen factory in

---

[1] Sir Charles Hanbury-Williams, *Isabella* (1740).

1709, Saint-Cloud was the only porcelain manufacture in Europe. Its fame long survived its effectual eclipse by Meissen, as the verse quoted above shows. In England, in the early part of the eighteenth century, Saint-Cloud porcelain was still sought after. Lady Mary Wortley Montagu, writing to the Countess of Mar in June, 1721, says: "My little commission is hardly worth speaking of; if you have not already laid out that small sum in Saint-Cloud ware, I had rather have it in plain lutestring of any colour." By this date, however, Meissen had long since taken the lead as Europe's foremost manufacture. Not only was its porcelain true "hard-paste", but its artists, both modellers and painters, were evolving a truly European and original style which was destined to become the model for all the factories which succeeded it. At the same time, however, Meissen was obliged in many things to copy closely the oriental wares which were, when all was said and done, the popular criterion of what porcelain should be. When the English factories were started, they found themselves bound by the same considerations, and were constrained to follow the models supplied by the Far East and by Meissen. The first of these factories were Chelsea (in production by 1745 at latest), Bow (perhaps started in 1744, certainly by 1748) and Bristol (founded in 1749 and transferred to Worcester by 1752). The Derby factory was in production by 1750, and a manufacture was founded about the same time at Longton Hall, in Staffordshire. All these factories made "soft-paste" porcelain, but two of them used bodies which differed from those evolved in France. Bow used the ashes of calcined bones, a strengthening element in the paste which was subsequently taken up at Chelsea and Derby, and which ultimately became the distinguishing feature of a specifically English type of porcelain – the "bone-china" of the nineteenth-century factories. The Bristol–Worcester concern added to its paste an admixture of soapstone (steatite), which produced a body better able than the normal soft-pastes to resist sudden changes of temperature. This was an obvious advantage in the production of tea- and coffee-wares, and a writer of 1763 already realized this clearly when he wrote: "I have seen porcelain of all the manufactures in Europe. Those of Dresden in Poland, and Chantillon (sc. Chantilly) in France, are well known for their elegance and beauty: with these I may class our own of Chelsea, which is scarce inferior to any of the others; but these are calculated rather for ornament than use, and if they were equally useful with the Oriental China, they could yet be used but by few, because they are sold at high prices. We have indeed, here, many other manufactories of porcelain which are sold at a cheaper rate than any that is imported; but, except the Worcester, they all wear brown, and are subject to crack, especially the glazing, by boiling water: the Worcester has a good body, scarce inferior to that of Eastern China, it is equally tough, and its glazing never cracks or scales off."[1] Soapstone porcelain of the Worcester type was made later also at Liverpool.

Of all the English factories, Chelsea, as the above quotation suggests, was held

[1] Annual Register, 1763, p. 104.

in the highest esteem, then as now. Apart from the beauty of its white paste and glaze, which have a quality all their own, its painters and modellers were of the highest class, and its manager a man of originality as well as of taste. Although Japanese designs were freely copied (sometimes perhaps from the Meissen copies!), and sometimes Chinese *famille rose* patterns, in a palette wholly unknown to that class of porcelain; and although the factory's first European flower- and figure-subjects (Pl. 24C) were closely derived from Meissen, it also made porcelain in styles entirely its own (Pl. 24D). The proprietor and manager, Nicholas Sprimont, was a silversmith by training, and a number of early Chelsea designs were such as might equally well have been executed in silver (and some were): in this, the factory shared a source of inspiration with Meissen, without in any way being dependent on it. To the naturalistic flowers which evolved at Meissen from the more formal European flowers in the manner of Klinger (cf. Pl. 24C), Chelsea added a decoration of large-scale flowers and plants derived from actual botanical examples (known by contemporaries as "Sir Hans Sloane's Plants"). Tureens in the form of animals, birds or vegetables are a commonplace in the porcelain and faïence of the eighteenth century, but none excel in humour of conception or beauty of execution the tureens made at Chelsea (Pl. 23B). Lastly, the Chelsea factory produced innumerable small *bibelots* or "toys" which have no equal in the work of any other manufacture. These, mainly scent-bottles, *étuis*, seal-hafts, patch-boxes and *bonbonnières* (Pl. 31A), seem to have been made pre-eminently as gifts, witty tokens in the elaborate game of eighteenth-century love-making. As such, their subjects are slily chosen. Cupid as kettle-drummer plays on a pair of breasts; minute *amorini* work away at a scent-flask made in the form of a forge of hearts; or the ubiquitous Cupid, seated on a pedestal, holds a globe inscribed JE TIENS LE MONDE, and so forms a haft for a carnelian intaglio inscribed FIDELLE. The scent-bottles were contained in shagreen cases and were often carried by ladies on coach journeys. These little trifles frequently bear such inscriptions, often in amusingly mis-spelled French – JE VOUS COFFRE (for "l'offre") or JE LE 'N PORTERAI.[1]

The Bow factory, less accomplished, nevertheless produced porcelain which at its best is of high quality (Pl. 23C). Apart from its numerous copies and adaptations of Japanese "Kakiemon" designs (Pl. 24B), it evolved a charming, characteristic palette of its own, and a style of soft flower-painting which is peculiar to it and very pleasing (Pl. 24A). Beyond this, it takes the credit for being the first English factory to introduce over-glaze printing into its decorative repertoire, although this process only developed fully at the Worcester factory (Pl. 23D). The obvious advantages of this process in the quick production of repetitive designs was quickly realized, and transfer-printing became common for the decoration of Liverpool porcelain and cream-coloured earthenware of all sorts during the third quarter of the century. The Derby factory was more remarkable for its figures (see below, p. 43) than for its table-wares, whilst the Longton Hall factory, although capable

---

[1] See G. E. Bryant, *The Chelsea Porcelain Toys*, London, 1925.

of charming and individual work (Pl. 23A), was too short-lived, and on the whole too dependent on Chelsea and other styles, to encompass any very notable achievements.

By a sequence of historical accidents, European porcelain in the eighteenth century was more than a mere material in which to make pleasing and convenient table-wares. It had been the custom in Germany, from as early as the fifteenth century, to deck out the tables at banquets with allegorical and symbolic scenes, the figures and properties of which were modelled in wax or in sugar confectionery. This vogue continued throughout the sixteenth and seventeenth centuries, and survived well into the eighteenth. It was therefore almost inevitable that an attempt should be made to supply these adjuncts of the table in the same material as that used for the table-wares. This natural impulse was brought to its full realization mainly by the genius of one man, the modeller J. J. Kaendler, who from 1731 onwards exercised an ever-growing influence at the Meissen factory. The development of porcelain figure-making, both technically and artistically, was extraordinarily rapid. From the small stiff and doll-like early figures on the one hand, and the slightly later large effigies of animals, saints and so forth on the other, there was during the 1730's a swift improvement in the modelling of smaller figures suitable for table decoration. By the time the English factories came on the scene, in the 1740's, there were innumerable Meissen models available for copying, and it is known that Sir Charles Hanbury-Williams, who had been English Ambassador at Dresden, in 1751 lent pieces of Meissen porcelain to the Chelsea factory for this purpose. It is certain that a number of the Chelsea models of the "red-anchor" period (about 1755) are direct imitations of Meissen prototypes. By 1754 the Chelsea factory was able to insert in the *Public Advertiser* a notice: "To be sold by Auction. ... The large, valuable, and entire Stock of the CHELSEA PORCELAINE, brought from the Manufactory there and the Warehouse in Pall-Mall; consisting of Epargnes and Services for Deserts, beautiful Groups of Figures, etc. ...".

In 1748 Sir Charles Hanbury-Williams had drawn up a list of "Figures to adorn the Middle of the Desert", in which different types of figures were systematically set out. The first fifty-four items were of a pastoral character, the next thirty-four had to do with hunting, the next four with everyday occupations; then came thirty-two figures of an allegorical character, followed by ten of foreign types. English figures very largely reflect these groupings, and a study of the Chelsea *Catalogues* of 1755 and 1756 shows how frequently figures within the different groups were lotted up together. Amongst the commonest types were "abstractions" of all sorts – the *Continents*, the *Elements*, the *Senses*, the *Seasons* (Pl. 22C) and so on, but Chelsea in particular evolved a beautiful series, partly original, partly copied from Meissen, in which figures of everyday life were portrayed (Pl. 22B). Mythological (Pl. 22D) and allegorical figures were common, whilst characters from the Italian comedy and representations of foreign peoples (Pl. 22A) appealed to the contemporary taste for the exotic. The final result, when from the store of figures available a grand assemblage was laid out, is brilliantly brought before our eyes by Horace Walpole in an essay written for *The World* of 8 February 1753:

"Jellies, biscuits, sugar-plumbs, and creams have long given way to harlequins, gondoliers, Turks, Chinese, and shepherdesses of Saxon China. But these, unconnected and only seeming to wander among groves of curled paper and silk flowers, were soon discovered to be too insipid and unmeaning. By degrees whole meadows of cattle, of the same brittle materials, spread themselves over the whole table; cottages rose in sugar, and temples in barley-sugar; pigmy Neptunes in cars of cockleshells [Pl. 22D] triumphed over oceans of looking glass or seas of silver tissue, and at length the whole system of Ovid's metamorphosis succeeded to all the transformations which Chloe and other great professors had introduced into the science of hieroglyphic eating. Confectioners found their trade moulder away, while toymen and china-shops were the only fashionable purveyors of the last stage of polite entertainments. Women of the first quality came home from Chenevix's laden with dolls and babies, not for their children, but their housekeeper. At last even these puerile puppet-shows are sinking into disuse, and more manly ways of concluding our repasts are stablished. Gigantic figures succeed to pigmies; and if the present taste continues, Rysbrack, and other neglected statuaries, who might have adorned Grecian salons, though not Grecian desserts, may come into vogue."

LATE GEORGIAN

THE decade immediately following the first half of the eighteenth century may be regarded as a period at which the ceramic craft of England, having emerged from the pre-porcelain era, was about to establish itself on a basis that would enable it to play no small part in the movement which, during the next 50 years, was to effect the gradual transformation of this country from a rural into an industrial community.

We have seen that the setting up of factories making soft-paste porcelain at Bow and Chelsea, from about 1745 onwards, was soon followed by undertakings at Bristol, Worcester, Derby, Longton Hall, and Liverpool, all of which, unlike their principal rivals at Meissen and Sèvres, relied on private enterprise rather than Royal patronage for their establishment.

In Staffordshire the coming of the china factories had imparted a fresh impetus to the making of earthenware figures and other wares, for, whereas the earlier potters had created a style whose charm lay in its native character and lack of sophistication, a new movement was now beginning which, gaining in scope and strength, was to bring Staffordshire, through the innovations of Josiah Wedgwood, an international market that has survived to the present day. It does not of course follow that the productions of the second half of the century were in an aesthetic sense superior to those of the first. In many respects quite the reverse is true. Names like those of Wedgwood, Thomas Whieldon, and the Wood family of Burslem, Ralph senior, his brother Aaron and their sons Ralph junior and Enoch, are associated with the highest standards of craftsmanship, but it must be remembered that all these, with the exception of the two younger Woods, were born and reared in the traditions of the earlier potters. Wedgwood alone was responsible for the great changes that were soon to take place. The population of England and Wales was rising, due largely, as G. M. Trevelyan points out in his *English Social History*, to "The Act of 1751" which placed a high tax on spirits and forbade their sale by distillers and shopkeepers. Not only did this do much to counteract the terrible ravages caused by the drinking of cheap gin, but also helped to popularize tea as a national beverage, which, after the middle years of the century, became a formidable rival to alcohol with all classes both in town and country. Porcelain was a costly material to produce and no doubt the potters of Staffordshire and elsewhere found an increasing demand for tea equipages which were within the means of the less well-to-do. Figures too, both human and animal, had greatly increased in popularity, principally as a result of importations from the Continent, especially Meissen, and imitations made by the English porcelain factories.

The makers of the traditional salt and lead-glazed wares had now to adapt their production to meet these new demands, and it was perhaps unfortunate that they found it necessary to seek inspiration from the more sophisticated styles of foreign Courts and Graeco-Roman art rather than pursuing their native craft within the sphere of its own limitations.

Salt-glazed stoneware had, since the beginning of the century, been a staple product of the potteries, and the use of plaster-of-Paris moulds (already described in the previous chapter) made possible the casting of such pieces by means of pouring the liquid clay slip into the mould and allowing the porous surface of the plaster to absorb the moisture. The mould was then removed and the piece made ready for firing. Hollow vessels were cast in this way while dishes, lids, etc., were made by pressing a flat piece of clay into the surface of the mould. These methods greatly facilitated increased production and by the middle of the century salt-glazed ware had obtained a considerable market, some being exported to Holland. Two Dutchmen settling at Hot Lane, now Cobridge, are supposed to have introduced into this country the "on-glaze" enamel painting with which, in a further attempt to emulate porcelain, much of it was decorated after 1750. This form of painting adopted by local artists was of various types and employed a strikingly contrasting palette including intense blues, pinks and greens. Besides Chinese themes, floral subjects and coloured grounds were used, presumably in imitation of Sèvres. Commemorative pieces include teapots celebrating the wedding of George III in 1761 and portraits of popular figures such as Frederick the Great, at that time an ally of this country. Figures of various subjects, mostly inspired by Meissen originals, are known (on the evidence of his account book) to have been painted with enamel colours in the Kentish Town workshop of William Duesbury, later proprietor of the Derby Porcelain Factory. At Liverpool, transfer printing, generally of a brick-red colour, was applied with most pleasing effects by Saddler and Green. Two figures of Turks (Pl. 25A) of about 1760 are illustrative of the influence of porcelain, being more or less direct copies of models made by J. J. Kaendler at Meissen in 1745. William Read in his *Staffordshire Pottery Figures* states that the models in question were probably made at Longton Hall by William Littler. They are also known in Bow porcelain. Another method of decorating salt-glazed pieces (referred to in the previous chapter) was by filling incised patterns with blue colouring, a type known to collectors as "scratch-blue".

In spite of the fact that this ware continued to be made for more than twenty years after 1750, it is not really typical of the period. Its extreme hardness and slightly abrasive surface, which scratched silver, rendered it less agreeable to public taste by comparison with the cream-coloured wares perfected by Wedgwood, and by 1770 its manufacture had largely declined, ceasing altogether before 1790.

We may at this point mention another class which, like salt-glaze, was to become outmoded by the use of new materials, namely the tin-glazed earthenware made principally at Lambeth, Bristol and Liverpool and known as English delftware. The development of this type in the first half of the century is dealt with in the previous chapter. In addition to the variety of objects made for domestic purposes already described there, a large number of tiles was also made (Pl. 26A), a typical feature of some eighteenth-century houses being a recess lined with such tiles and containing a ceremonial washbasin and water bottle. They were also used in the surrounds of fireplaces and for lining the walls of larders and shops.[1] Dated inscriptions occur frequently, also political slogans and the recording of events such as Lunardi's balloon ascent in 1783. In spite of the latter date delftware had largely gone out of fashion by the last quarter of the century, and like salt-glaze was not made after 1790.

As we have already seen, it is in many instances quite impossible to draw an arbitrary date line within which we may state what is characteristic of one half of a century and not of the other. Many types are transitional, and it is therefore only possible to note their production during the particular period with which we are dealing. In this category must be included the mottled or tortoiseshell wares chiefly associated with the name of the Staffordshire potter Thomas Whieldon (see p. 35). These mottled effects were brought about by the blending of metallic oxides in a clear lead-glaze which was applied over a cream earthenware body. Manganese produced the rich madder-brown of the tortoiseshell, while other colours were obtained by the use of oxides of copper, iron and cobalt which caused brown, green, yellow, blue, purple and grey tones to mingle in the fluid glaze with pleasantly harmonious effects. Glazes stained with either a single colour, or in the various combinations described above, were used on pieces with both applied and moulded reliefs. They include teapots, coffee-pots, tea-caddies and the whole range of table wares. Figures, both human and animal, were also coloured in this way. The teapots and similar pieces sometimes show evidence of the silversmith's influence (Pl. 25B), while the later figures were in many instances suggested by foreign originals. They are, nevertheless, unmistakably the work of a native craftsman, and as such no doubt found their way on to the shelves and mantelpieces of the local homesteads. Under the present heading mention may also be made again of the agate or marbled effects obtained by the blending of various coloured clays, as described in the last chapter. In the "solid agate" these clays were used to form the body, but marbling was also simulated by applying them over a plain surface. A brilliant black glaze on red earthenware is also typical. It is often seen on tea and coffee-pots ornamented with small reliefs. The same shapes, together with a

[1] See "An Introduction to Bristol Delftware Tiles", by Louis Lipski, *The Connoisseur*, May 1953.

similar glaze, were also used at Jackfield in Shropshire (see p. 36), though the latter type is without relief decoration.

During his partnership with Whieldon, Wedgwood was continually experimenting with both technical and material improvements made in order to stimulate an increased demand for their products, as in spite of reduced prices lack of public interest had already been reflected in a steadily declining market. Among these improvements was the perfecting of a green glaze which he used in combination with yellow on teapots and other vessels made in imitation of fruit and vegetable forms, the "Cauliflower" and "Pineapple" wares already referred to (see p. 36). Although excavations on the site of his factory show that Whieldon made the whole range of Staffordshire pottery favoured in his day, his productions were not marked. His fame as a potter, however, has caused a whole class to be identified with his name. He was a man of great integrity, and before his death in 1795 became Sheriff of his county.

The name of the Wood family is to many only connected with the making of Toby Jugs. They were, in fact, extremely versatile in their output. Of the two elder brothers, Aaron (already referred to in the last chapter) was the most celebrated "block cutter" of his time, that is, he prepared the first intaglio moulds in alabaster or other hard substance from which, after the taking of a master cast, the plaster moulds already described were eventually obtained. He worked for most of the leading Staffordshire potters, including Whieldon, and was probably at some time in partnership with his brother Ralph. As already mentioned (p. 39), he is credited with the making of some of the most interesting figures of which the so-called "Pew Groups" are notable examples. Aaron's brother, Ralph (born 1715), and his son, Ralph junior (born 1748), besides making useful wares were, from about 1765 onwards, responsible for a large output of figures coloured in the Whieldon style. It is generally agreed, however, that they themselves were principally concerned with the technicalities of manufacture rather than the creation of the types for which their name has become famous, and the best of the later models are confidently attributed to an itinerant artist of French extraction named Voyez. John Voyez was born about 1740 and was trained as a jeweller. On first coming to London he worked for a time at this trade and also as a carver for an artificial stone manufactury, exhibiting work in both wax and artificial stone at the Society of Artists in London, 1767–8. Josiah Wedgwood was originally responsible for bringing him to Staffordshire in 1768, but his habits were totally at variance with the former's high standards of moral rectitude, and after his disorderly conduct had led to a term of imprisonment their association terminated abruptly, though Wedgwood thought so highly of Voyez's abilities that he tried to deny his services to rival potters by bribing him not to work for them.[1] But Voyez was not to be tempted and is known on the evidence of signed pieces to have worked for both Humphrey Palmer of Hanley and T. Hales of Cobridge. His association with the

[1] See Herbert Read's *Staffordshire Pottery Figures*, London, 1924.

Wood factory is based on stylistic grounds, as no examples are known which bear both his signature and Ralph Wood's factory mark. The grotesque vessels known as Toby Jugs are perfect examples of rural English pottery of this period, adorning as they did the chimney pieces of farm houses and cottages. It is thought that their original form was inspired by engravings of "Toby Philpot", the subject of a song called "The Brown Jug" translated from the Latin by Francis Fawkes and published in 1761. The subjects are, however, considerably varied, names being applied to them such as "The Thin Man", "The Planter", "Martha Gunn", "Prince Hal" (Pl. 26c), etc. In the catalogue of the late Captain Price's collection it is suggested that the last named represents George IV, when Prince of Wales, mas-

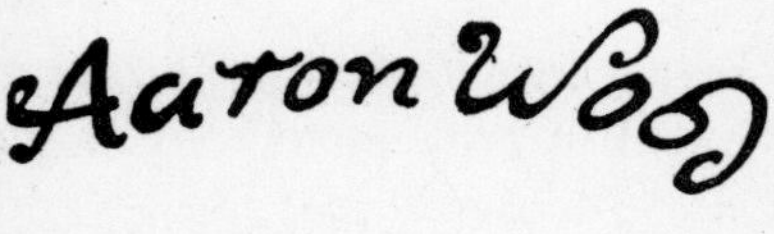

Incised

Fig. 6. On a "block" in the British Museum.

1   2   3

All Impressed

Fig. 7. 1 and 2 are believed to be the marks of R. Wood senior. 2 is supposed to be a rebus on the family name. About 1770. 3 is believed to be the mark of R. Wood junior. 1772–95.

Impressed

Fig. 8. Signature on a "Fair Hebe" jug.

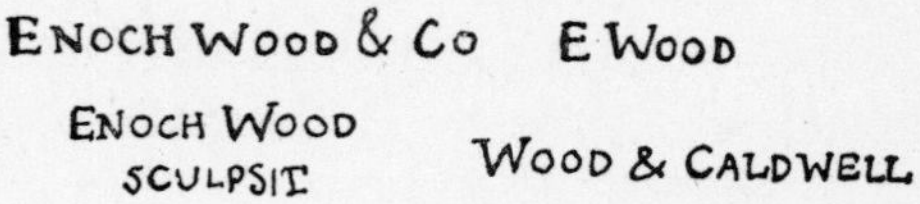

All Impressed

Fig. 9. Marks used by Enoch Wood. His partnership with Caldwell was from 1790 to 1818.

querading at a Brighton ball as Bluff King Hal. Toby Jugs were made by other potters besides the Woods, and have continued to the present day, generally with steadily declining merit. Well known examples of Voyez's work are the rustic jugs moulded in the form of a tree trunk with figures in relief, and an inscription "Fair Hebe" (Pl. 26B). These are often signed and dated 1788.[1] Other figures from the Ralph Wood factory include copies of originals by Paul Louis Cefflé of Luneville, musicians, pastoral and classical subjects and satirical groups such as "The Vicar and Moses" in a double-decked pulpit. In addition to colouring in the Whieldon style the Woods developed a method of laying the metallic oxides on under the glaze into which they were partly absorbed, a technique that produced beautiful and characteristic effects. The elder Ralph died in 1772, and his son in 1795.

Enoch (born 1759) was the son of the blockcutter Aaron. He was in partnership with his cousin from 1783–90, and James Caldwell from 1790–1818. Enoch was a

[1] The author had in his possession an example stamped with the mark ASTBURY, indicating that it was made by R. M. Astbury, who directed a factory at Fenton, 1785–1800.

D

modeller on his own account though his work lacks distinction. A number of busts such as those of George Washington and the preachers Whitfield and Wesley are the best known examples. The latter was modelled from life in 1781. He also made figures, some of which are of considerable size.

During this later period the practice already used by the china factories of painting in opaque enamel colours over the glaze was adopted. This lacked the charm of the earlier methods and has not proved practical, as the colours usually flake off with the passing of time. Enoch, who did not die until 1840, came to be known as the "Father of the Potteries".

Some critics have accused Wedgwood of spoiling a native art by turning it into a manufacture and urging his employees to desert nature and seek inspiration in examples created by an archaic civilization; but these criticisms, although undoubtedly merited in some respects, do less than justice if they cause us to ignore his mighty achievements both in the field of technical improvement and in the setting up of a great industry demanding the highest standards, not only in the materials used but in the craftsmanship applied to them. Even the most individual spirits cannot remain uninfluenced by the tastes and fashions of their times, and in this respect Wedgwood was not the creator of the neo-classical movement, though he found himself in complete harmony with the aims and ideals of its devotees. Although as a potter he may not have been a great creative artist, he was undoubtedly an extremely competent one; and it is surely remarkable that a man who had received only an elementary education should have been able to engage successfully in experiments that today would be regarded as the work of highly skilled experts.

A man of strong social and moral convictions, his sympathies lay with the American Colonies in their fight for independence. He also joined the campaign for the abolition of slavery. A medallion of a slave in black and white Jasper ware, modelled at the factory by William Hackwood, and inscribed "Am I not a man and a brother" was adopted as the seal of the Slave Emancipation Society, of which Wedgwood was a keen supporter. Yet in spite of these activities his achievements secured for him the highest social contacts, including the frequent patronage of Royalty. The *London Ledger*, 1793–1806, shows an order placed by Queen Charlotte in 1795, listed[1] as follows:

12 Milkpans	6 Dog Pans
Sundries	3 Dog Pans
18 Plates Green Ivy	Silver Spout
	Teapot
2 Teapots	Jasper Vases and
	Gerandoles
6 Plates Green Ivy	2 Toy Tea Sets
	Sandwich Set

[1] *Catalogue of Early Wedgwood Pottery Exhibition,* Josiah Wedgwood & Sons, 1951.

Born in 1730 at Burslem in Staffordshire, Josiah Wedgwood was, at the age of 14, apprenticed to his brother Thomas who had inherited the family business known as the Churchyard Pottery. His apprenticeship lasted for five years, but it seems unlikely that he left the Churchyard before 1752, when he went to Stoke and entered into a partnership with John Harrison at the factory of Thomas Alders. This does not appear to have been of long duration and was followed, as we have seen, by his association with Whieldon from 1754–9. During this time he accumulated sufficient capital and experience to set up on his own account at the Ivy House, Burslem, where he continued to produce the Whieldon types with improvements in the shapes and glazes. Being a man of great foresight and business acumen, he was quick to realize that these were already declining in popularity, and to see before him the possibility of capturing a large market if he could offer to the public something which should be without the practical disadvantages of salt-glaze and at the same time of a sufficiently stable body and colour to be produced in large quantities at a price that would make it available to all classes. To this end he set about a further refining of the cream-coloured earthenware body used by Whieldon and the earlier potters. His business premises were extended in 1764 to include the neighbouring Brick House Works, later known as The Bell House, and by 1765 he had so far progressed in the making of cream ware as to obtain the patronage of Queen Charlotte and the right to name his new product Queensware, a type which with continued improvements was to capture a world market. The early factory decoration of Queensware is of a simple classical style, but much was sold in the white to be painted elsewhere, as well as being sent to Liverpool for transfer printing by Saddler and Green. It was readily adaptable to every kind of use and Wedgwood made from it articles ranging from dairy and culinary equipment to the Imperial Russian Service, consisting of 952 pieces, made in 1773 to the order of the Empress Catherine II and known as the "Frog Service", owing to the fact that it was to be placed in the Palace of La Grenouille near St Petersburg and has the device of a green frog in a shield painted on the border of each piece (Pl. 27A). It is further decorated with English views in dark purple monochrome. The eventual cost of this service was about £3,500, on which only a small profit was made.

While visiting Liverpool in 1762 Wedgwood first met the merchant Thomas Bentley, who, it is said, inspired him with his love for the antique. The friendship and mutual interest between the two men grew steadily, and in 1768 a partnership was decided upon and Wedgwood commenced the building of the great manufactory just outside Burslem which he named "Etruria", Greek vases at that time being thought Etruscan. In the same year he opened a large London showroom in Newport Street.

The partnership with Bentley was for the making of ornamental pieces only, the ordinary wares continuing for a few more years to be made at the Bell House. By 1769 the premises at "Etruria" were completed and opened, and Wedgwood was now fairly launched on his projects to emulate the examples of antiquity.

In his search for materials other than the cream and marble bodies suitable for this purpose, he had once again made use of a local product, namely the black unglazed pottery known as "Egyptian Black". This he improved and refined to obtain a fine quality black stoneware of extreme hardness from which he made many vases and other pieces, naming them "Black Basaltes". Some of these vases, in addition to being decorated with engine turning, were bronzed with light gilding,

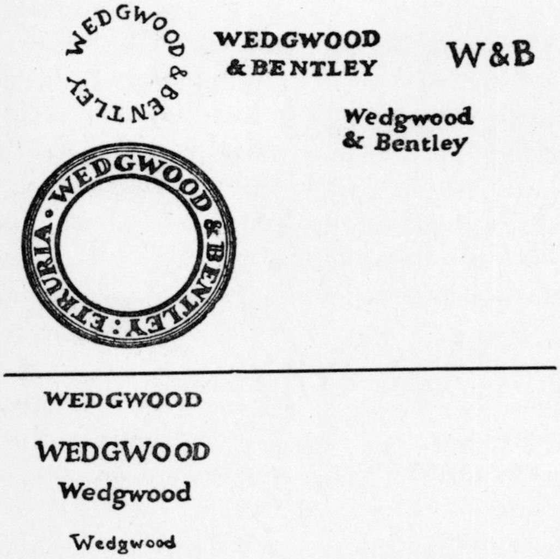

WEDGWOOD & BENTLEY

W & B

Wedgwood & Bentley

WEDGWOOD

WEDGWOOD

Wedgwood

Wedgwood

Fig. 10. Specimens of the marks generally used by Wedgwood. Those above the line are of the Wedgwood and Bentley period, 1769–80; those below are later marks, from 1771 on useful wares, and from 1780 onwards on all classes. The mark was of various sizes, the letters being sometimes in upper and sometimes lower case. All impressed.

Fig. 11. Impressed on a scroll. Late eighteenth and early nineteenth century.

NEALE & Co

NEALE & WILSON

WILSON

Fig. 12. The marks of Neale & Co. and Neale & Wilson. Late eighteenth and early nineteenth century. All impressed.

and others painted with "encaustic" enamel in imitation of Greek vases. The latter work was probably done at an enamelling establishment opened in Chelsea in 1769 under the supervision of Thomas Bentley. The Frog Service was certainly painted there. Besides the usual domestic articles a series of busts for library decoration were made in black basaltes, also figures; that of Voltaire (Pl. 28A) made about 1777 is a well-known example. It was also used for the making of small relief medallions to meet the current vogue for collecting cameos in cabinets; the originals being too costly for the ordinary purse, most people had to be contented with imitations made in inexpensive materials. Among other unglazed bodies were the buff-coloured "cane ware" and a red stoneware called by Wedgwood "rosso antico". It is interesting to note that, at the beginning of the nineteenth century, the scarcity of flour was so acute that imitation pie-crusts made of cane ware were used to suggest the real thing.

Best known of all Wedgwood's creations are the coloured ground or "jasper" wares, and one has only to think of a room designed by Robert Adam to realize how admirably suited they were to the surroundings in which they were so often incorporated.

Once again the problems of composition arose and were solved by patient research and experiment. A pure white stoneware capable of tinting throughout with oxides was the basic requirement for the making of the coloured bodies and white reliefs. Barium sulphate obtained in a mineral form from Derbyshire, where it was called "cawk", was found to be the necessary ingredient, and by the end of 1775 jasper was being made in two or three shades. The range was soon increased and instead of being tinted throughout the pieces were immersed in a solution that coloured the outer surface only, referred to as "jasper dip". The most usual colour is light blue; a darker blue, two shades of green, lavender, lilac, black and rarely yellow were also used; while for the famous copies of the "Barberini" or "Portland Vase", started in 1786, the body was of a blue-black "solid jasper" in imitation of the glass from which the original was made.

Many of the forms in jasper repeat those of the black basaltes and are too well known to warrant description. It was, however, put to innumerable uses. Wedgwood himself lists 38 different items in a single order made by a merchant in Manchester for supply to the King of Naples,[1] from which the following examples are taken:

Rings.	Coach Panels.
Snuff Boxes.	Swords.
Window Shutters.	Chairs.
Metal Boxes.	Cabinets.
Door Handles.	Watches.
Buffets.	Desks.
Chest of Drawers.	Metal Lamps.
Chatelaines.	Buckles.
Etui Cases.	Daggers.
Bell Pulls.	Opera Glasses.
Smelling Bottles, etc.	Coat Buttons.

The metal work on pieces mounted in ormolu and cut steel jewellery (Pl. 28B) was carried out by the Birmingham metal workers Boulton & Watt, with whom Wedgwood was constantly in touch.

About 1780 a white semi-porcellaneous version of the Queensware was perfected and named "Pearl Ware". This was used largely for services made in competition with the china makers. Silver and coloured lustres also came into use in

[1] See Wolf Mankowitz, *Wedgwood*, London, 1953, p. 108.

the late eighteenth and early nineteenth century. A well-known example is the pink variety often found on services made in the shape of shells. Enamel painting in the Chinese style on the black basaltes was also done, though the combination appears entirely incongruous.

Wedgwood was tireless in his efforts to obtain not only the highest standards of workmanship but also to seek out the best examples of antiquity which could be adapted to his uses. To this end he employed many well-known artists and craftsmen, as well as gaining access to famous collections such as that of the Duke of Marlborough. James Tassie, well known for his casts of antique gems, worked for him, also John Flaxman, the famous sculptor, who, together with Henry Webber, spent some time in Rome supervising the making of reductions and adaptations from the antique for use at the factory. The wax modellers, Mathew and Isaac Gosset, are known to have worked on a series of contemporary celebrities known as the "Illustrious Moderns", with William Hackwood, for many years principal modeller at the factory. Besides the work of professionals, some charming designs in relief of women and children are attributed to Lady Templetown, Lady Diana Beauclerke and a Miss Crewe. George Stubbs, the celebrated animal and portrait painter, who was a friend of Wedgwood's, also designed a number of relief medallions of equestrian subjects. Many other names are known, but space forbids their inclusion here. All work was subject to Wedgwood's supervision, being altered or adapted at his discretion, and this, together with the fact that names of individual artists were rarely allowed to appear, sometimes makes personal attributions largely conjectural.

Thomas Bentley died in 1780 and in 1790 Wedgwood's three surviving sons, John, Josiah and Thomas and his nephew, Thomas Byerley, were taken into partnership. Within three years, however, Wedgwood senior, Josiah II and Byerley alone remained. In 1795 the founder himself died and Byerley in 1810.

It was inevitable that, as the creator of new materials and forms of ceramic expression, Wedgwood should have a host of followers. The Queensware was copied by most of the potters of his time, and even rivalled in quality; notably by that made at Leeds in Yorkshire; while the jaspers, besides inspiring local imitators such as William Adams, John Turner and Samuel Hollins, compelled even the great Continental factories of Sèvres and Meissen to follow the English example.

The pottery industry from the Midlands to north of the Border was now well on the way to complete industrialization and therefore largely stereotyped in its products. The figures of John Walton, with their clumsy tree-stump supports and vivid green foliage, are obvious copies of Chelsea Derby porcelain, but a certain degree of originality is shown in the blue, green and orange palette of the so-called Pratt wares, while the firm of J. Neale & Co., later Neale & Wilson, made figures and table wares of good quality, often tastefully painted with bright enamel colours. Fresh inspiration was, however, lacking, and the nineteenth century produced no innovators capable of leading a new revival.

Porcelain. Unlike earthenware, English porcelain had no roots in the national tradition. It was a new and untried medium with high costs and hazards of production that caused its makers to cater essentially for the tastes of the fashionable and monied classes rather than the humbler sections of the community.

The first porcelain seen in Europe was imported from China and was so highly prized that attempts were continually made to discover the secrets of its composition, the great distinction being its whiteness and translucency compared to the dense opacity of earthenware.

In the sixteenth and late seventeenth centuries soft paste or artificial bodies were achieved in Italy and France, but true porcelain in the Chinese sense was not made in Europe until Johann Friedrich Böttger, working at Meissen in 1700 (see previous chapter), discovered the secret of compounding china clay (kaolin) with china stone (petuntse). These, when fired at a high temperature, combine to form the hard vitrified material known as hard paste or true porcelain. This discovery, which was of immense financial value, was jealously guarded, Böttger being kept a virtual prisoner by Augustus the Strong, Elector of Saxony, under

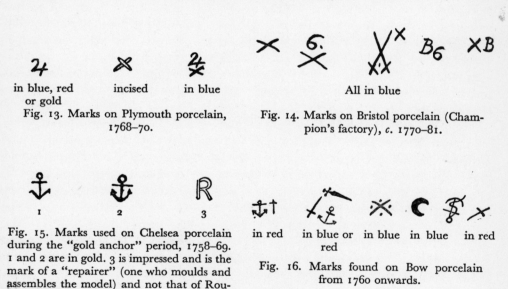

in blue, red   incised   in blue
or gold

Fig. 13. Marks on Plymouth porcelain, 1768–70.

All in blue

Fig. 14. Marks on Bristol porcelain (Champion's factory), c. 1770–81.

Fig. 15. Marks used on Chelsea porcelain during the "gold anchor" period, 1758–69. 1 and 2 are in gold. 3 is impressed and is the mark of a "repairer" (one who moulds and assembles the model) and not that of Roubiliac the sculptor as is sometimes supposed.

in red   in blue or   in blue   in blue   in red
          red

Fig. 16. Marks found on Bow porcelain from 1760 onwards.

whose patronage the great German factory near Dresden was established in 1710.

In England no such discovery was forthcoming and, with the exception of that made by William Cookworthy at Plymouth 1768–70, and later by Champion of Bristol, who sold the patent to New Hall, all English porcelain was of the soft paste variety. In the foregoing circumstances it was inevitable that Meissen, or Dresden china as it is better known, should become the model on which the first

English styles were based, the majority being close imitations; though silver was also copied, particularly at Chelsea. Early English porcelain is, by reason of its paste, glaze and restrained decoration, of a quality equal to anything made elsewhere. By 1760, however, the baroque force of Meissen had given way to the rococo extravagances of the royal factory at Sèvres. Nowhere was this change more apparent than at the Chelsea factory, where the proprietor, Nicholas Sprimont, had inaugurated the final phase of production, known from the mark used, as the "gold anchor" period (1758–70). Previously figures made in England had, like their German counterparts, been designed for use principally as table decorations and therefore could be viewed from any angle. Now, however, they had become popular as garnitures for mantelpieces and china cabinets, and the simple mound bases gave way to rococo scroll work mounted on feet, a design more suggestive of ormolu than porcelain. These bases were picked out in bright colours and gilding, while trees with branching foliage and flowers (bocage) often formed the background against which the figures were set, either singly, or as groups, the largest and most famous of the latter being the "Music Lesson" (Pl. 29) taken from a painting by Boucher. Other groups of unusual size are a "Roman Charity" and a pietà, while the best of the single figures include two finely modelled Harvesters (Pl. 32A), a set of Apollo and the Muses and another set known as the Ranelagh Masqueraders.

The diarist[1] Mrs Philip Lybbe Powys, who wrote during the years 1756 to 1808, and who gives a glimpse of the domestic activities of the upper classes of those days, does not fail to mention china collections. "Lady Dashwood's china-room," she observed after a visit in 1778 to Kirklington Park, "is the most elegant I ever saw. 'Tis under the flight of stairs going into the garden; it's ornamented with the finest pieces of the oldest china, and the recesses and shelves painted pea-green and white, the edges being green in a mosaic pattern. Her Ladyship said she must try my judgement in china, as she ever did all the visitors of that closet, as there was one piece there so much superior to the others. I thought myself fortunate that a prodigious fine old Japan dish almost at once struck my eye."

A large and more splendid collection was at Blenheim. It delighted the Duchess of Northumberland when she saw it in 1752: "We were also shown a little China Room, very prettily fitted up in wᶜʰ is the China presented by the K. of Poland to the present Duke." This china closet was not the one which the indefatigable Mrs Lybbe Powys saw at Blenheim in 1799: "I went in the post-chaise to Blenheim, to see the new china-rooms. They are not in the house, but built just after you enter the park, four little rooms fill'd with all sorts of old china fix'd to the walls by three screws, one of which takes out to let them be removed, others are placed on pedestals or shelves. The whole has a pretty effect, but to others might be more amusing than to Lady Hardy and myself, as each of us has most of the same sort." The Blenheim "China Gallery" was fitted up in 1796, "an additional

[1] Quoted in "The China Case and China Closet", by R. W. Symonds, *The Connoisseur*, June 1952, p. 11.

attraction to the visitors of Blenheim, who delight in the antique, rich, and curious specimens of the porcelain, delf, and japan manufacture".[1]

The ground colours of Sèvres were also imitated, such as the "gros bleu" (called "mazarine" blue), a rich claret (contemporarily "crimson"), also green, turquoise and yellow. Typical examples of these ground colours are seen on the sets of elaborate rococo vases lavishly gilded and painted with figure subjects after Rubens, Boucher and Teniers. *Chinoiseries* in the style of Watteau and Pillement were also popular, together with birds, flowers and fruit. Famous among the vases is the claret-ground set of seven, once in the possession of Lord Dudley and now in Lord Bearsted's collection.[2] They are painted with mythological subjects and birds in the manner of Hondecoeter. The Huntington Art Gallery in California also possesses a fine pair and they are well represented in the British and Victoria and Albert Museums.

The table wares were no less magnificent in their ground colours and painting; a superb example is a tea and coffee service, the bequest of Emily Thompson, which may be seen at the Victoria and Albert Museum. Even more elaborate is the enormous equipage given in 1763 by George III and Queen Charlotte to the latter's brother, the Duke of Mecklenburg-Strelitz. It is mentioned by Horace Walpole as consisting of "dishes, plates without number, an epergne [Pl. 32B], candlesticks, salt-cellars, sauceboats and tea and coffee equipages costing £1,200". He adds, however, "I cannot boast of our taste; the forms are neither new, beautiful, nor various. Yet Sprimont the manufacturer is a Frenchman. It seems their taste will not bear transplanting." This service, which is decorated with exotic birds and flowers within mazarine blue and gilt borders, is now in the private collection of H.M. Queen Elizabeth, the Queen Mother; but a damaged pair of candelabra was sold by the steward of the Duke's household and is in the Schreiber collection at South Kensington. In the private collection of Her Majesty the Queen are two remarkable clocks with claret grounds, gilt scroll work and pastoral figures in the style of Boucher.

In 1769 Sprimont sold the factory to James Cox who, in the following year, resold it to William Duesbury and John Heath of Derby. Duesbury continued for a number of years to use the premises, the productions of this period being known as Chelsea-Derby. They are, in most cases, somewhat insipid in character and not typical of the best of either factory. The table wares usually follow the style of

---

[1] It seems obvious that the above cannot refer to English porcelain. In the first paragraph Mrs Lybbe Powys is speaking of a visit to a porcelain-room which she made in 1778, and states that it is "ornamented with the finest pieces of the oldest china": this could hardly apply to English porcelain made only twenty or thirty years previously, and the "fine old Japan dish" was probably oriental. In the second paragraph the Duchess of Northumberland's visit to Blenheim was in 1752, and the "K. of Poland" was the Elector of Saxony, owner of the Meissen factory: it would seem, therefore, that whatever porcelain he gave to the Duke of Marlborough most likely came from that establishment. The "delf" is presumably Delft, and would be tin-glazed earthenware, while that of "Japan manufacture" would, again, be oriental.

[2] On loan to the Victoria and Albert Museum.

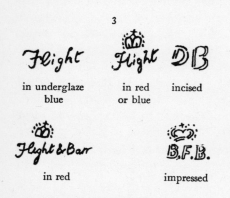

1

in underglaze blue

2

Rd.Worcester   R.H.f

R. Hancock fecit Worcester

All in black

3

Flight   Flight   DB

in underglaze   in red   incised
blue   or blue

Flight & Barr   B.F.B.

in red   impressed

Chamberlains
Worcs No 276

in red

Fig. 17. Marks on Worcester porcelain. 1 and 2 were used during the Dr Wall period, 1752–83. The pseudo-Oriental characters occur on pieces of the "Japan patterns", about 1760–75, and the crossed swords are in imitation of Meissen; the number is sometimes 91. The fretted square is of Chinese origin. 2 shows the marks of Robert Hancock found on transfer printed pieces. The anchor is thought to be a rebus on the name of Richard Holdship, who was in charge of the printing department: it also occurs on pieces signed in full by Hancock. 3 shows the marks of the late eighteenth and early nineteenth century.

1   2   3   4
in gold   in gold   in blue,   incised
or red   puce or gold

5   6
in blue,   in puce
puce or red

7

All incised

Fig. 18. Derby factory marks. 1 is usual on Chelsea-Derby porcelain, 1770–84. 2 is about 1770–80. 3 is about 1780–4. 4 is incised on figures 1770–80. 5 is about 1784–1810, the red mark is late. 6 is the mark of Duesbury and Kean, about 1795. 7 shows marks incised on figures 1770–1800, they are the catalogue numbers of the model. The symbols are those of "repairers".

Fig. 19. Staffordshire pottery cock and hen, late eighteenth century. 8¼" and 7¾". *Schreiber Collection in Victoria and Albert Museum.*

decoration favoured by the neo-classical revival, while the figures are pale echoes of their predecessors. In 1784 the factory was finally closed and the moulds and workmen removed to Derby.

Although Bow ranks with Chelsea as the first of the great factories, very little of any consequence or originality was made there after 1760. The rococo style prevailed in the forms, which were similar to those of Chelsea, while much of the bright colouring was probably applied outside the factory. One of the owners, Wetherby, died in 1762, and his partner, John Crowther, went bankrupt in the following year. After this the history becomes obscure. Like Chelsea, it was probably financed by Duesbury and removed to Derby about 1775. A valuable contribution to the making of porcelain which originated at Bow was the use of bone ash in the paste (see p. 41). This made production less hazardous as it stabilized the body and helped to prevent collapsing in the kiln.

Of the early factories, Longton Hall closed in 1760, and only three, Worcester, Derby and Lowestoft, survived into the nineteenth century. The two former are still flourishing, but Lowestoft closed in 1802. This Suffolk factory could lay claim to few of the pretensions of its rivals. Its wares were for the most part of a utilitarian character and catered for a less opulent market. Many pieces bear scenes and inscriptions relating to the locality, typical examples being the well-known inkwells, mugs, etc., inscribed "a Trifle from Lowestoft". No recognized marks were used, and owing to the publication of a notorious mistake much Chinese export porcelain has been wrongly attributed to this source.

Worcester, during its best period (1751–83), was under the direction of Dr Wall, the founder, and William Davis, a partner and manager. The figures made there were negligible both in quantity and quality, but in the sphere of table wares, vases, etc., their work was unsurpassed.

One invention which, although it did not originate at the factory, was more widely practised there than elsewhere, was transfer printing, chiefly in black, over the glaze. This method, of which Robert Hancock the engraver was the chief exponent, may be claimed as an original English contribution to ceramic art. It was used at Worcester from about 1757 onwards and forms an interesting group, mainly depicting the scenes and customs of the time. Armorial and commemorative pieces were also made, the best known of the latter being the signed and dated mugs with portraits of the King of Prussia (Pl. 30A). *Chinoiseries* in the manner of Pillement were another feature.

In 1769 there was a migration of workers from Chelsea to Worcester, after which the rich ground colours and gilding of the former factory predominated in the more ambitious productions. Coloured fish-scale grounds, ultimately derived from Meissen, were also a great feature, blue being the most usual. They are often seen in combination with exotic birds (the "fantasie vögel" of Meissen) painted in panels (Pl. 30B). Oriental influences appear in the so-called "Japan patterns" and various *chinoiseries*, the neo-classical style coming later.

A number of celebrated services were made, to which the name of distinguished patrons have been attached. One of the best known is supposed to have been made for William Henry, Duke of Gloucester. It is painted in the centre with large clusters of fruit within gilt and green borders intersected by compartments with sprays of fruit and insects.

The best known painters of Worcester porcelain are John Donaldson, the miniaturist, and Jeffrey Hamet O'Neale. Much outside decoration was also done in the London workshop of James Giles.

After the death of Dr Wall in 1776 and William Davis in 1783, various changes in ownership and partners caused the firm to come successively under the management of Thomas Flight, Flight and Barr, and Barr Flight & Barr, the last partnership ending in 1813. Robert Chamberlain, another member of the firm, having seceded in 1789, set up first as a decorator and later a manufacturer in opposition. The last phase is characterized by the somewhat pompous Empire style favoured in the early nineteenth century.

The great beauty attained in the early days at Derby was not fulfilled during the middle period. Many figures were made, some depicting contemporary notabilities; that of David Garrick in the character of King Richard III is a familiar example. This was modelled from an engraving by J. Dixon, published in 1772, after the painting by Nathaniel Dance, exhibited in the Royal Academy in 1771. In most instances, however, Meissen was once again the source of inspiration. The colours are generally bright, a dry turquoise blue, which tended to discolour and become brown, being particularly characteristic. The Continental influence is further seen in a class of white, unglazed biscuit groups intended to imitate marble, which were a speciality of the factory. One of the first and most important works in this medium is grouped as three figures representing the Royal Family after a painting by Zoffany (Pl. 31B). The only complete set known is in the possession of Her Majesty the Queen. Some of the later models are by J. J. Spengler, son of the director of the Zürich Porcelain factory, who was at Derby from 1790–5.

Decoration on the later table wares, vases, etc., was of a very high standard and many talented artists were at work. Zachariah Boreman painted landscapes, James Banford and John and Robert Brewer figures, landscapes and other subjects, while the naturalistic flowers of William Billingsley and William Pegg (Pl. 27B) are notable, as are the pink monochromes in the Sèvres style by Richard Askew, and the birds of Complin. Others were Fidèle Duvivier, Lawton and Hill.

William Duesbury died in 1786 and was succeeded by his son of the same name who, in 1795, took a miniature painter, Michael Kean, into partnership. The second Duesbury died in the following year and Kean carried on the factory until 1811.

Outside the main areas porcelain was also made at Coalport in Shropshire and Pinxton in Derbyshire, as well as at Liverpool. But by the end of the eighteenth century the greater part of the industry was concentrated in Staffordshire.

REGENCY

The Countess of Granville in the autumn of 1810 wrote: "Dinner [for the earl and herself] consisted of soup, fish, fricassée of chicken, cutlets, veal, hare, vegetables of all kinds, tart, melon, pineapple, grapes, peaches, nectarines with wine in proportion. Six servants wait upon us, a gentleman-in-waiting and a fat old housekeeper hovering round the door. Four hours later the door opens and in is pushed a supper of the same proportion."

Silver, plate, china and cut-glass for such a meal was equally profuse: when guests were present the amount tabled was prodigious. Butlers now stored their silver in strong rooms, although in old-fashioned establishments the plate was returned to chests deposited in the trunk room adjoining the master's bedroom.

China and glass not in daily use was stored in the china closet. Tiers of shelves to the ceiling displayed gleaming surfaces of glaze painted with rich, lustrous enamels. Many of these treasures were, of course, inherited: soft paste porcelains potted at Bow, Chelsea, Derby and Worcester, and fine earthenwares from Wedgwood and Spode. By 1810 these had been joined by bone china and the so-called semi-porcelains such as stone china (Pl. 33A) and felspar porcelain (Pl. 33B). These were fashionably enamelled with the family coat-of-arms in full colours, or might display fantastic birds with long tails and crested top-knots, among flowers of impossible colour and form; fierce dragons with knobbly claws and rolling eyes; rivers thickly sprinkled with tiny, fairy boats; English scenes and mansions among homely meadows and heavy trees. Every room in the house, too, was garnished with china, ranging from vestibule vases, capacious fish globes, and pastille burners to toilet sets in the dressing rooms.

It has become customary to decry English ceramics of the early nineteenth century. Those who do so fail to appreciate their technical excellence. Improved methods produced stronger and more colourful ware capable of giving enduring service yet within purse reach of the general public. The pottery industry was revolutionized and Britain dominated world markets for the next hundred years.

Bone china (Pls. 34A, B, and 36B) was the most important of the new ceramics, replacing as it did the soft porcelains. It was brought to perfection by Josiah Spode in the early 1790's, and ledgers still in existence prove it to have been on sale in

1794 under the name of British Cornish china. The term china was eventually deemed unsatisfactory, as for almost half a century it had been associated in the public mind with the more fragile soft porcelains. Josiah Spode II, then, in 1810, under pressure from his partner, William Copeland, renamed their British Cornish china, calling it Stoke porcelain. When in 1814 Spode (Pls. 33A; 35B, 36B; 36A, 37B) was appointed potter to the Prince of Wales he was cited as "Potter and Manufacturer of Stoke Porcelain". Bone china is a late Victorian trade name.

Domestic ware in bone china gave enduring service, and its glaze was such that overglaze colours sank into it permanently and did not flake. Enamelling became a less hazardous process and the intense fusion produced a less painted-looking finish. Greater brilliance in the hue of the enamel was possible after 1812 when Samuel Walker's high temperature enamelling kiln replaced the small box muffle in which ware had been baked without exposing it to direct contact with the flames. Hitherto it had been customary for purchasers to select their patterns from the china-seller's sheets of hand-painted designs. The dealer then commissioned an independent enameller to decorate the service, which had been bought from the potter in the white. The introduction of the enamelling kiln now meant that much more domestic ware was painted in the factory than formerly.

Oriental designs adapted to the English taste were ornamenting bone china table services by 1805 and had become the height of fashion by 1810. If analysed such patterns may appear more essentially Chinese than Japanese, although a superficial resemblance to Imari porcelain has led to their classification as Japanese. Less numerous on table services were decorations of the Kakiemon type. The Shanghai pattern by Spode was of Chinese inspiration and copied by other Staffordshire potters using the old muffle enamelling process on bone china badly flawed with specks. Although the Chinese influence on table services declined during the 1820's there was a distinct vogue for patterns in the Imari style, with flowers and shrubbery in vivid colours surrounded by gilt tracery.

Hard, translucent felspar porcelain, again a Spode invention, enriched many a nobleman's table in the form of magnificent dinner services in which the centre of each piece expansively displayed in full colours the owner's coat of arms (Pl. 33B) and the rims were radiant with heavily gilded ornament. Sometimes an old gold colour replaced gilding, its effect being considered more in harmony with the enamelled armorial design. Dessert services in felspar porcelain might bear painted landscapes with titles, and borders of conventional flowers. Stone china (Pl. 33A), a felspathic earthenware of delicate grey-blue body, which emitted a clear ring when lightly tapped, was ornamented with old Chinese designs. Extensive table services in this ware were in great demand.

Families at this time were large and entertainment lavish. Dinner services were standardized to twelve covers, but frequently extended to thirty-six, with thirty serving dishes for game and meat. Plates for the three main courses were of the same size and the service also included soup plates. Dinner and dessert services combined became fashionable, the pieces matching. These ranged from soup and vegetable tureens to shell-shaped dessert dishes and dessert plates. The old practice of serving dessert on ware of a different type and pattern continued, however. A typical family service contained a pair of tazze, four dishes and twelve plates.

Special services were evolved for supper and from about 1815 were made up of about 130 separate pieces: four fan-shaped dishes and covers, four square dishes and covers, one octagonal dish, liner and cover, two sauce tureens and stands, with ladles, two oval egg-stands each with twelve egg cups, six octagonal meat dishes, four oval dishes, a salad bowl, twenty-four each of soup, dinner and dessert plates. The combined tea and coffee set with but a single set of saucers now gave way to one with a full complement of saucers.

The late Georgian period was the heyday of blue-and-white transfer-printed domestic ware (Pl. 35B), from table services to toilet accessories, in bone china and in earthenware. The majority were made in Staffordshire, many at Leeds and on Tyneside. Fine tone gradations were achieved by 1810 by combining line and stipple engraving on a single copper-plate. Skilful use of light and shade resulted for the first time in well-balanced pictures, clear in detail, yet covering every part of the ware, thus concealing surface flaws in the fabric which in consequence was of a cheaper quality than that needed for enamel painted decoration.

Blues became more brilliant from about 1816 when the close of the Napoleonic wars made it possible once more to import fine Saxon cobalt. Shades of blue were now given such trade names as Canton, zaffres, glowing blue, willow blue, mazarine, and flower-blue. The war-time English cobalt blues and synthetic blues continued in use but only on the cheapest earthenwares. In 1828 it was discovered that certain crushed enamel colours mixed with barbados tar would, like cobalt, print direct to the fired but unglazed ware known as the biscuit, without distorting during glazing. These were various tints of green, red and yellow, but although they had a few years of popularity they failed to oust Staffordshire blue.

Transferred subjects had been derived formerly from Chinese blue and white. These gave way from about 1810 in favour of purely English subjects. Dinner and tea services presented the English scene with imaginative enthusiasm – the beauty spots, cathedrals, cities and resorts then considered to qualify as picturesque views. Staffordshire blue was not intended for use on formal occasions, but for daily service in the home, its pattern being protected by the glaze.

Each flat piece in a Staffordshire blue table service, every dish, plate, sauceboat and gravy-tray displayed a picture. Each piece of hollow-ware, whether jug, vegetable dish or sugar-bowl, carried three or four differing scenes on its inner and outer surfaces. At least twelve pictures belonging to a series would decorate a table service, but as many as seventy-two have been noted on a dinner service illustrating the travels of Dr Syntax. Between 1816 and 1830 the list of potters specializing in blue-printed ware exceeded fifty, in addition to the transfer-print departments operated by several of the great potters.

A glimpse of the large amount of miscellaneous ware that might be stored in the china closet was extracted from the Spode ledgers of this period by Arthur Hayden. Included were artichoke cups, asparagus trays, broth bowls, butter tubs and stands, card racks, chamber candlesticks with extinguishers, cheese dishes, cheese toasters, chestnut vases, chicken tureens, custard cups, cylinder pin-cases to screw, ice-pails, inkstands and pen-trays, match-pots, mugs, radish trays, roll-trays, root-dishes, rouge-pots, salad bowls, sandwich sets, scent-jars, snuff-boxes, snuffer trays, steak-dishes with compartments, strawberry baskets, sugar boxes, supper plates, syrup pots, toast racks, turtle pans, violet baskets and wafer boxes. Punch and toddy bowls ranging from two gallon to quart capacity were bought in matching sets. It was customary for these drinks to be served hot, hence the tall foot rim for protecting the table surface from heat.

Ironstone china, patented by Charles James Mason in 1813, was a hard earthenware capable of development far beyond the range of table-ware, for which it was eminently suitable. Sets of bedposts, enormous vases for drawing-rooms and vestibules, huge wine cooling cisterns and goldfish globes were made as well as fireplaces in full- and half-size. Fireplaces, typically, were finished with a white-glazed ground enriched with trailing leaf-patterns in gold and panels of flower and foliage sprays in pink, puce, pale green, apple green, vermilion, blue. Panel ornament differed in each; flowers included peonies, full blown roses, hawthorn sprigs and daisies, all with their foliage, as well as dragonflies, butterflies and other flying creatures. It was Mason who evolved the celebrated jugs which bear his name and appear to have been in unceasing production since. These octagonal jugs with snake handles and colours of sparkling brilliance were issued in sets of a dozen sizes. Their low price precluded high quality in decoration and finish.

The Napoleonic style in ornamental ceramics is recorded in pattern books of 1810, with such features as the plinth base with lion-paw feet. Details were sumptuously gilded, often with scroll-work in low relief, as evolved in 1802 by Henry Daniel. Solid grounds in burnished or matt gold, and grounds of gold scale on blue and of stippled gold were fashionable. Increased domestic illumination from oil-lamp and gas-chandelier made the most of this brilliance. The revived rococo style of the silversmiths was adopted by Coalport and Rockingham and within five years every leading potter had followed their example.

Pictorial reserves (Pls. 34A and 34B; 35B and 36B), from about 1815, tended towards the English rural style with such border motifs as birds, landscapes, flowers, fruit, shells and feathers. These were usually painted on the white against such ground colours as dark and scale blues, apple green, yellowish green, deep yellow, canary yellow, greyish turquoise, marbled brown, marbled blue, crimson, salmon, lavender and cane colour. Designs favoured half a century earlier by Chelsea and Worcester were revived, and much of this bone china now masquerades as soft porcelain in the cabinets of collectors. The claret ground with bird decoration in gold, a Chelsea style, was widely copied, the finest coming from Spode, but even his ground colour failed to reach Chelsea's full splendour until the 1830's. Spode did succeed, however, in reproducing the *gros bleu* of Dr Wall's Worcester, although in the salmon-scale ground his blue was livelier than the original.

George IV as Regent and as King was an extravagant collector of pre-Revolution Sèvres porcelain. He established a vogue that made the French ware so scarce that by 1815 it was almost unobtainable. The trade in Sèvres for decorating the home became so profitable that any expedient was used for acquiring supplies. These was a demand, long in vain, for an English potter capable of reproducing old-style Sèvres complete with the famous double-L monogram. In 1825 Thomas Randall established a pottery for this purpose at Madeley in Shropshire, but refused to forge the Sèvres mark. His productions were virtually indistinguishable from Sèvres, and many china cabinets of the period and today preserve old Madeley instead of Sèvres. Consignments of Madeley porcelain are known to have been sent to Dover and from there despatched to London as fresh arrivals from Parisian dealers.

The finely modelled figures in soft porcelain that had formerly decorated pier tables and wall brackets and had been grouped at the centre of dining and dessert tables, were now superseded by ostentatious vases, singly, in pairs or in garnitures of three or five. Three tall urns flanked by a pair of pot-pourri vases decorated in a matching design constituted a drawing-room vogue of the period and in the late 1820's these might be centred by a clock set in a flamboyant flower-encrusted case of bone china.

For drawing-rooms, entrance halls and passages there were massive covered vases in bone china, sometimes exceeding a yard in height, supported on separate pedestals rimmed with pierced galleries of ormolu. Oval *jardinières* might have a dark blue ground with rims encircled in non-repeating flower patterns and mounted with elaborate ormolu work. Some vases early in the period displayed Moorish characteristics in their richly gilt arabesque patterns. Later vases with a *bleu de roi* ground were enriched with reserves containing meticulously painted pictorial scenes or copies of French paintings.

Ceramic figures (Pls. 38c and 40B) were made in vast quantities, but these were mainly in earthenware and found no place in the fashionable home unless in kitchen or servants' quarters. The Derby factory continued making the figures that had brought wealth to Duesbury in the eighteenth century, but now in bone china. These were more lively and of greater charm than any competing figures until the 1830's. There was little enough to recommend them, however, beyond a general gaudy splendour.

The general public, nevertheless, clamoured for the crudely formed, garishly coloured earthenware figures issued in many tens of thousands each year and sold in the streets from a tray of twenty or thirty specimens balanced upon the hawker's head. A prolific maker of these was John Walton of Burslem, using a cheap, brittle earthenware capable of high-speed moulding. Almost every small home in the

E

country possessed a few of these colourful trifles costing only a few pence each. Ralph Salt of Hanley specialized in the rather more costly *bocage* pieces, sporting dogs, and sheep with hand-raised wool: these had a country-wide sale. Among the twenty other potters producing figures at this time was Obadiah Sherratt of Hot Lane, who made some popular large chimneypiece ornaments; his "Politos Menagerie" of about 1816 was considered a triumph of casting and firing (see p. 72).

Any home of pretension, no matter what its size, ensured that every room was sweet-smelling in those days of perfunctory sanitation by using pastille burners. Such a burner from about 1820 might be in the form of a bone-china or earthenware cottage containing a slowly smouldering perfumed cone composed of powdered willow-wood charcoal, benzoin, perfumed oils and gum arabic. These cottages represented old-world dwellings surrounded by gay flower-beds, minute coloured flowers encrusting the walls and edging the roof, with gilt chimneys from which curled the pastille's scented fumes. There were also turreted castle gateways, circular toll houses with conical roofs, clock towers, thatched farm-houses with flowery arbours, and many another rustic building.

Night-light shelters in the form of cottages immediately followed the invention of the self-consuming candle-wick in 1825. Faint, unflickering light from a short, thick mortar candle that did not require periodic snuffing glowed from the cut-out windows. The tiny flame was well-protected against draughts, too, and was a source of flame in those days of laborious flint-striking.

Lithophane night-light shelters date from 1828. These pictorial transparencies were made from a thin, glassy hard porcelain and gave the effect of detailed mezzotints by precise variations in the thickness and consequent opacity of the material. Lithophanes were also used as firescreens and panels for hall lanterns. Even teacups with enamelled decoration on their sides might surprise the visiting users with lithophanes in their bases, the pictures becoming visible as the cups were tilted against the light.

Food warmers, catalogued as pap-warmers, performed the duties of night-light shelter as well as keeping hot liquids warm enough to drink during the night. These vessels were in three parts: pedestal, loose cup and cover. The pedestal was an open-sided cylinder fitted with a mortar which acted as a source of heat and a night-light. Fitting loosely into its open top was a round-based covered cup. The pedestal top from about 1825 might be made in a piece with a deep inner bowl for containing boiling water. Into this fitted the covered drinking cup. This was still heated by a mortar. At about the same time appeared tea warmers in bone china and porcelain (Pl. 35c). The fully enclosed pedestal held a teapot, the whole being enamelled to match the tea service.

The scintillating glints of lustre ware began to enliven the living-rooms and kitchens of lesser homes during this period and even tea services were decorated with films of lustrous metal. Silver lustre, obtained from platinum oxide, was introduced by the Wedgwood firm in 1805, but the all-over form which made earthenware resemble sterling silver plate or plated ware began its astonishing vogue in 1823.

Stencilled effects were evolved by John Davenport in 1806, but little was made until 1810, when it met with the competition of silver resist lustre. In the same years Peter Warburton of New Hall patented a method of transfer-printing in gold and silver lustre. Moonlight effects, now known as marbling, were introduced in the same year. Later came the mottled pink lustre of Sunderland (Pl. 35A).

Mocha ware, so named because of its resemblance to the quartz mocha stone, was in demand for kitchen jugs and mugs and large cups and saucers after its invention about 1780. Its base was of cream-coloured earthenware. The shaped clay was covered with chestnut brown, green or yellow slip: over this was applied a slip in contrasting colour – usually brown, but green, blue and black might be used – mixed with tobacco and hops. This spread into patterns suggestive of trees, feathers and moss. From about 1830 a stronger base was used, either white earthenware or cane-coloured stoneware.

Dipped ware was also a favoured decoration for inexpensive but colourful kitchen earthenware. This consisted of hollow-ware in which slips of three colours – blue, brown and yellow – were applied to the biscuit. Skilful workers could produce attractive bands, stripes, spots, curves and spirals at great speed. The ware was fitted into a lathe and, when revolving, slips were poured into a three-sectioned funnel, emerging from adjoining openings and held in such a way that a fine stream of tri-coloured slip flowed upon it.

A list of major potters is given below.

The principal products of the leading Regency potters

NAME OF POTTERY	DATE OF ESTAB.	CERAMICS POTTED 1810–1830
Adams (Stoke-upon-Trent)	1790's	cream-coloured earthenware; basalt; stoneware; bone china from 1816
Coalport	1795	bone china; felspar porcelain from 1822
Davenport	1795	earthenware; cream-coloured earthenware; bone china; stone china; lustre ware from c. 1820
Derby (Bloor from 1815)	1749	bone china
Herculaneum (Liverpool)	1800	bone china; earthenware
Madeley	1825	soft paste porcelain
Mason	1797	earthenware; bone china; stone china; ironstone china from 1813
Minton	1793	earthenware; bone china
Nantgarw & Swansea	1813	soft paste porcelain and soapstone porcelain until 1823

Fig. 20. Spode's "Grasshopper" pattern: the transfer for a six-inch tea plate taken from the original engraved copper plates. *Spode-Copeland Museum.*

New Hall	1781	hard paste porcelain to about 1810; bone china from 1810
Ridgway	1802	fine earthenware; stone china; bone china
Rockingham (Brameld)	1807	cream-coloured earthenware; stone ware; bone china from 1820
Spode	1776	earthenware; bone china; felspar porcelain; stone china; new stone china from 1810
Swansea (Cambrian Pottery)	1769	earthenware; cream-coloured earthenware; stone china; lustre ware from early 1820's (see Nantgarw)
Wedgwood	1759	earthenware; cream-coloured earthenware; basalt; un-glazed earthenware; bone china 1812–1822
Worcester	1751	bone china

With the exception of Madeley and Nantgarw, all the above issued blue and white transfer printed ware. There were also twenty other makers of bone china in Staffordshire listed in 1818. Earthenware potters in 1820 numbered at least a hundred, established in Staffordshire, Yorkshire, Sunderland, London, Derbyshire and elsewhere. Some of the more important of these were Joseph Stubbs, Enoch Wood, Clews, Rogers, of Staffordshire; Joseph Bourne of Denby; Doulton at Lambeth.

EARLY VICTORIAN

AMONG the multiplicity of wares which poured from the British potteries during the three decades 1830–60 a broad distinction can be made between those of a popular nature which tended to persist in traditional forms and those of a more sophisticated appeal which readily reflected the complexities of contemporary fashions. The conservatism of the popular wares can be seen especially in the slip-ware of the country potteries, the mocha and other more industrialized slip-wares, the saltglazed stoneware, the lustre ware and the "ironstone china" with derived oriental patterns. Such wares continued into or through the Early Victorian period, but their manufacture was mainly associated with style which had been defined and popularized at an earlier date.

Printed and painted earthenwares. The transfer-printed earthenware, which was at the height of its popularity in the years around 1830, showed largely the same conservatism in an established popular style. A great part of its manufacture was designed for export, and through the 'thirties and 'forties it was made by almost every factory of importance in Staffordshire, and by several elsewhere. The use of fanciful scenes, and of actual scenes in this country, in America and else-where, continued as central motifs in the printed patterns. In the border decora-tions rococo foliage and scrollwork tended to become increasingly common, and this is particularly noticeable in the printed ware from Copelands (the Spode factory, known as "Copeland and Garrett" from 1833 to 1847, and then "W.T. Copeland, late Spode") (Pl. 39A). From Wedgwoods came some excellent over-all floral patterns.

Blue remained the most popular colour for underglaze transfer-printing; but from the mid-'twenties other colours were frequently used, and in the 'thirties and 'forties these included black and varying shades of red, green, yellow, brown and purple. The more expensive method of overglaze printing, by transfer from gela-tine "bats" instead of paper, was used where fine detail was required; and this proved especially useful for the delineation of the multitudinous girders of the 1851 Crystal Palace on souvenir ware of that year. Multi-coloured underglaze printing appeared in the later 'forties. Some particularly successful work of this nature was

Fig. 21. A vase by Antoine Vechte of Hunt and Roskell.
Inscribed: ANTOINE VECHTE FECIT 1847.
The Worshipful Company of Goldsmiths.

produced by Jesse Austin for the firm of F. and R. Pratt of Fenton. Colour-printing was much used by this firm for the decoration of jar lids, and it was used also on tablewares such as those which were shown at the 1851 Exhibition and which earned the firm a prize medal. The colour-printed tablewares were made chiefly for export to America, where they were still being sold in the 'nineties.

Painted decoration on earthenware tended increasingly to follow the styles of porcelain painting; and this was particularly true of painting on the new hard earthenwares which were being developed as imitations of porcelain. Some notable work, although largely in a porcelain style of painting, was being carried out during the 'thirties and 'forties, and later, by William Fifield Junior on the cream-coloured ware of Rings of Bristol. At Wedgwoods bold over-all patterns were produced in a more appropriately earthenware style, which are reminiscent of the same firm's printed floral patterns; and the earlier Wedgwood mode of painting in opaque colours on a black ground was taken up in the harshly coloured productions of the Lowesby pottery in Leicestershire about 1835.

Pottery figures. Pottery figures were made in great quantities during the period, and like most of the popular wares their styles show relatively slight changes from those which were in vogue earlier in the century. It is noticeable, however, that pottery figures tended increasingly to diverge in style and subject-matter from those made in porcelain (which will be described later). Made mostly by back-street potters in the Staffordshire pottery towns, the early Victorian pottery figures were destined for the most unsophisticated market and show to a surprising degree the simple vigour and ingenuousness of a "peasant" art. Among the work of this nature produced in the years around 1830 two main types are prominent. One is that of John Walton and his followers, which seems to belong most typically to the 'twenties; of his followers working in the following decade or so the best known is Ralph Salt who used lustre decoration as well as enamel colours (see p. 66). The second prominent type of figure-work is one which is thought to be associated with Obadiah Sherratt (also see p. 66). It is characterized by a curious table base with bracket feet on which are placed groups depicting bullbaiting or else crudely humorous scenes. Much of this work is probably of the 'twenties, but that it continued at least into the middle 'thirties is shown by the use of the new word "teetotal" in the title of a group illustrating the advantages of sobriety.[1] A later development was the "flat-back" type of figures, which were mostly left white with a sparing decoration in colours and gilding (Pl. 40B). These developed around the middle of the century and achieved great popularity in the 'fifties. Among the makers of these figures in Staffordshire the firm with which they have been mainly associated is that of Sampson Smith of Longton, which continued over a long period to make wares of this nature including pottery dogs for

[1] R. G. Haggar, *Apollo*, L., 1949, p. 146.

mantelpiece decoration. Flat-backs and other sorts of simple coloured figures were also made in Scotland at Prestonpans and elsewhere.

Other manifestations of Early Victorian work in a broad-based popular spirit were the small models of buildings, such as cottages and churches, and the spirit flasks formed into the shapes of human figures. Many of the model buildings were decorated with roughened patches of vegetation, which also appear on certain dog figures as patches of fur; such work is often described as "Rockingham", although most of it was probably made in Staffordshire.[1] The spirit flasks shaped into amusing or topical figures were intended for use in inns. They were greatly in vogue in the years around the passing of the Reform Act of 1832 with representations of the leading political figures of the time. In saltglazed stoneware they were made with other fancy wares by the firm of Bournes of Denby, by several small potteries in the Chesterfield district, and by firms in London, including Doultons of Lambeth. Elsewhere similar flasks were made also in earthenware covered with a brown so-called "Rockingham" glaze.

Fashionable wares. The wares described so far have been mainly popular wares, and most of them were made in styles which were comparatively long-lived. In contrast, the styles of the more fashionable wares are seen in this period to multiply rapidly and to affect different ceramic materials in differing degrees, so that the general pattern of stylistic changes becomes one of great complexity. The ceramic arts were closely affected by the new spirit of self-consciousness which was characteristic of the Victorian approach to the decorative arts and was expressed by the appearance of the Government Schools of Design in the late 'thirties and 'forties, by the beginning of circulating collections about 1844 from which the Victoria and Albert Museum was to develop, by the appearance of magazines such as the *Art-Union* and the *Journal of Design and Manufactures*, and, in 1851, by the first of the great international exhibitions. Perhaps the extreme instance of this new self-consciousness was Henry Cole's project of "Summerly's Art Manufactures", which was being worked out in 1847 and 1848. Inspired by his success in winning a Society of Arts award for a simple well-designed tea service made by Mintons (Pl. 43B), he tried the experiment of commissioning designs for useful objects, including pottery and glass, from well-known painters and sculptors, such as Richard Redgrave, H. J. Townsend and John Bell. That such an experiment was made, and was received with initial enthusiasm, is of greater significance than that the artists themselves were unable to rise to the occasion.

The Revived Rococo. In 1830, and during the following decade, the most significant style in English porcelain was that of the Revived Rococo. It had come as a reaction against the formal heavily-gilded French Empire style of the early years of the century and by the 'thirties was at the height of its development. It was

---

[1] W. B. Honey, *English Pottery and Porcelain*, 1947, p. 231.

scarcely a directly imitative style in the sense of copying precise examples of eighteenth-century porcelain. In effect it used motifs from the general resources of the eighteenth-century rococo style as a medium for expressing a sense of freedom and of a certain extravagant prettiness. Into this category came much of the more pretentious work of the Rockingham factory at Swinton, Yorkshire (which was closed in 1842). It appeared in the work of the Derby factory (closed in 1848) and of the Davenport factory at Longport; but probably the most significant work in this style was that carried out at the factory of John Rose at Coalport (often referred to at the time, and today, as "Coalbrookdale") (Pl. 41A).

Besides the use of scrollwork and the tendency towards asymmetrical forms which are implied by the title "rococo", the revived rococo made an extensive and characteristic use of applied flower-work. The great care and skill which was lavished on irregular groupings of flowers on the bodies of vessels, and on elaborate bouquets perched on lids, was in accordance with the Early Victorian respect for naturalism and greatly exceeded in botanical accuracy their eighteenth-century prototypes. In the 'forties the revived rococo style as such was on the wane, but the use of applied flowers continued, and the appearance of the new parian porcelain body in the later 'forties, with its marble-like qualities, led several manufacturers to use applied flower-work in the new body, unpainted and virtually unglazed. At the firm of Pountneys in Bristol Edward Raby was a notable specialist in applied flower-work who turned to parian in this way. The firm of Samuel Alcock of Burslem produced similar work; and at the 1851 Exhibition parian pieces with applied flower-work were shown by T. and R. Boote and T., J. and J. Mayer, both of Burslem. Such work in parian was clearly impractical for normal purposes, if only because of the difficulty of cleaning it, and comparatively little is heard of applied flower-work after the early 'fifties.

Relief decoration. One of the most characteristic products of the 'forties and early 'fifties was a group of wares with cast relief decoration. These were mainly jugs, but sometimes included also mugs and other similar objects. Many of the earlier examples of the jugs stand upon clearly differentiated feet; but in general they have loose sagging bodies with the weight well towards the base and wide upward-curving lips. The looseness of form was often accentuated by the great depth of the relief decoration, and this is in contrast to the comparatively shallow relief of Castleford and other earlier analogous wares. A number of different materials were used, varying from a putty-coloured earthenware to brown salt-glazed stoneware and parian porcelain, but most frequently and characteristically the material was some form of hard vitreous white ware which can usually be described as a fine stoneware. Sometimes the jugs were coloured throughout or were painted; sometimes, as in the case of many of those produced by the Samuel Alcock factory, the ground was coloured, leaving the relief decoration in white, or vice versa, to give somewhat the effect of jasper ware. On some of the jugs, particularly in the early 'forties, the decoration was in the Gothic taste, as on examples made by W. Ridgway and Son of Hanley in 1840 and Charles Meigh of Shelton, Hanley, in 1842 (Pl. 39B). Bacchanalian themes were popular, as in an example with which Charles Meigh won in 1847 a medal offered by the Society of Arts for a relief-ornamented mug (Pl. 39B). Others were of genre subjects, such

Fig. 22. Jug with painted relief decoration from the firm of John Ridgway, Shelton, about 1845. *Art-Union* (1846, 318).

Fig. 23. A classical jug by Copelands, from the Manchester Exhibition of 1845–6. *Art-Union* (1846, 32).

as the jug depicting a boy bird's-nesting shown by T., J. and J. Mayer in the 1851 exhibition, or subjects of contemporary commemorative interest, such as the "Distin" jug made by Samuel Alcock and by Cork and Edge of Burslem depicting a family of axhorn players who had given popular concerts in the Potteries.

Probably the most significant relief decorations, however, were the running plant patterns, consisting of long sprays or branches of a plant disposed about the surface of a vessel and originating usually from a rusticated handle. The use of these patterns was an expression of the same feeling for asymmetrical looseness and for naturalism as had inspired the revived rococo shapes and the use of applied flowers in porcelain; but with the important difference that whereas the applied flower decoration on elaborate revived rococo shapes tended to take the form of local embellishment, the running plant patterns were conceived in relation to the whole area to be decorated. A contemporary parallel to this treatment of plant patterns, and perhaps a source of inspiration, was the relief decoration on some of the French "Beauvais" stoneware, which was shown at the Paris Exhibition of 1844 and was publicized by the *Art-Union* of that year. The free and highly naturalistic early-Victorian style of running plant patterns seems to have developed about the middle 'forties, when it can be seen for instance in the 1846 *Art-Union* in illustrations of the work of the firm of John Ridgway of Cauldon Place, Shelton (Fig. 22). Besides the stoneware jugs and similar wares, it is noteworthy that this style appears also in relief decorated silverware and in engraved glassware. In parian porcelain the running patterns were used, particularly by Mintons, as cast relief decoration on a variety of objects, including even cups and saucers. It is interesting to notice that in the early 'fifties Mintons were also rendering these loose over-all patterns in applied flower-work on parian vases (Pl. 40A); and the style even appeared in jasper ware among Wedgwoods' collection at the Paris exhibition of 1855.

A similar, and more extreme, expression of the Early Victorian passion for naturalism was the use of Plant forms for the whole shape of ceramic objects. The whole form and surface of a vase, for instance, might be shaped to represent the leaves of a lily-of-the-valley plant with the flowers protruding from the sides. Such conceptions were by no means new in ceramic history; but the mid-nineteenth-century versions were not normally designed in an imitative spirit, and together with the running plant patterns the plant forms can be regarded as an original expression of the aesthetic ideas of the period. This again was a style which ceramics shared with work in silver and other media. In the years around 1849–51 a great deal of interesting and often beautiful work of this nature was produced in parian porcelain and other materials by such firms as Copelands, Mintons, Samuel Alcock and G. Grainger of Worcester.

"Majolica". Plant forms and heavy relief plant motifs of various sorts were also found to be appropriate in the Victorian version of "majolica", which was produced by Mintons just in time for the 1851 Exhibition. In the 1856 *Art-Journal* (the successor of the *Art-Union*) the Minton majolica is described as "one of the most successful revivals of modern pottery". It is said that Herbert Minton was inspired by green-glazed flower-pots which he had seen in Rouen in 1849; and the durable coloured-glaze ware which resulted was mainly developed by Léon Arnoux, a young French potter who was later to be art director of the factory. The ware was regarded at the time as an imitation of Italian "majolica", and in consequence the term (spelled with a "j") came to be attached to this type of pottery which has little connection with the true tin-glazed and painted "maiolica" of art history. Sometimes the Victorian majolica was painted, but usually the term was used merely to imply earthenware with coloured glaze or glazes. The heavy majolica, particularly with green glazes, was much used in forms incorporating large leaf shapes, as in the instance of a chestnut dish by Mintons (Pl. 43A); and this fashion led Wedgwoods to revive their own eighteenth-century use of green glaze in the production of dishes covered entirely with large-scale naturalistic foliage in relief. Majolica in this sense became the common medium for the innumerable Victorian *jardinières* with plant-form or other decoration in bold relief, which were made in Staffordshire potteries throughout the rest of the century and beyond.

Sèvres imitations. Alongside these stylistic developments in the free use of rococo motifs and natural forms, much imitative work was being carried out in porcelain in the manner of the eighteenth-century wares of Sèvres, Dresden and Chelsea. Of these the work in the manner of Sèvres was by far the most important and became one of the strongest elements in the later porcelain tradition of this country. Victorian imitations of this sort differed from the "revived rococo" in so far as the makers were serving an informed taste for the originals, and considerable efforts were therefore made to reproduce the original styles as exactly as possible. Admiration for Sèvres porcelain and the imitation of it had been virtually continuous in this country since the eighteenth century. In the 1830's much work in a distinctively Sèvres style was being carried out at Derby. During the 'forties it became the most fashionable style for the better class of porcelain at nearly all the leading factories, including particularly Roses of Coalport, Copelands and Mintons. The Coalport factory was the one which, under the influence of W. F. Rose from 1841, devoted the greatest amount of attention to the exact reproduction of the eighteenth-century Sèvres colours and decorations. In this the firm was also guided and encouraged by the important London dealers, Daniell and Co., whose name often appears on the wares. Great efforts were made to match the coloured grounds of the old Sèvres, and the Coalport versions of such grounds as "bleu de roi", "rose Pompadour" (mistakenly known at the time as "rose du Barry") and turquoise were regarded as triumphs of imitation. Some of the imitations made at Coalport, and elsewhere, were so exact as to include old Sèvres marks: a refinement which can scarcely have been carried out without any intention to defraud.

Porcelain painting. Porcelain painting naturally tended to follow the porcelain styles. It is noteworthy, however, that neither the revived rococo nor the Sèvres style offered such wide opportunities to the porcelain painter as had the French Empire style of the early years of the century, and it is perhaps for this reason that porcelain painting tended to become less interesting and less important during the early Victorian period. The revived rococo was largely concerned with surface modelling and with raised decoration, and only grudgingly accorded the flat areas which are required for composed "pictures" on porcelain objects. The Sèvres imitations were limiting to the porcelain painter to the extent that they implied the reproduction of a Sèvres manner of painting. By the 'thirties the lush naturalism, which had characterized the flower painting of the early part of the century, had given way in the work of some of the painters to a harder, more mannered and sharply coloured style. Flower painting of this sort, often against a dark ground, is associated particularly with the younger Steeles, the brothers Edwin and Horatio, who had been working at Derby and also, in the case of Edwin, at the Rockingham factory.[1] Similar work is also found from Coalport and from the factories in Staffordshire. The work of the 'forties and 'fifties in the Sèvres style led to carefully placed and over-precious painting, such as the flowers and trophies of William Cook of Coalport. Some interesting bird painting was also produced at Coalport in the eighteenth-century Chelsea manner. One of the more outstanding figure painters was Thomas Kirkby, whose finely painted amorini appeared on some of Mintons' porcelain at the 1851 Exhibition. Much of this artist's later work was carried out on the Minton majolica. Another accomplished figure painter was Thomas Bott of Worcester who became widely known in the later 'fifties and 'sixties for his white enamel painting on the "Limoges ware" of Kerr and Binns (the Worcester firm which succeeded to the Chamberlain factory in 1852 and was known as the Worcester Royal Porcelain Company from 1862) (Pl. 42A).

Classical and other influences. The mid-century Sèvres imitations in porcelain represented in some degree a bridge between rococo and classical sources of inspiration. The Victorian interest in classical work was not, however, derived from this source. To some extent the direct imitation of classical shape and decoration seems to have continued since the days of the first Josiah Wedgwood; but the greatly increased interest in this sort of work in the 'forties has something of the appearance of an intellectually-inspired movement which had little in common with the general aesthetic outlook of the period. In the mid-'forties writers in the *Art-Union* were repeatedly stressing the importance of Greek inspiration, which in the idiom of the time was described as "Etruscan" or "Etrurian". In the years around 1845 Copelands were producing a quantity of wares in direct imitation of Greek shapes and decorations, and were extending these ideas to such utilitarian objects as ewers and basins. In this phase the high-handled Greek "oenochoe" jug shape was especially favoured (Fig. 23). During the late 'forties L. L. Dillwyn's Swansea factory was producing its "Etruscan ware"; and Wedgwoods were reviving their eighteenth-century designs in jasper ware and black basaltes. In the same period, and in the 'fifties, the London firm of Thomas Battam made a speciality of imitative Greek wares, and at the 1851 Exhibition their display took the form of an artificial grotto meant to represent an "Etruscan tomb" overspilling with appropriate pottery.

[1] W. B. Honey, *Old English Porcelain*, 1948, p. 129.

Another aspect of the revival of classical ideas can be seen in the widespread fashion in the 'fifties for work in terracotta; that is, in highly-fired unglazed earthenware. Attention had been drawn to French work in this medium at the Paris Exhibition of 1849. The material was considered to be particularly suited to garden ornaments, and at the 1851 Exhibition an amount of large work of this nature, mostly in classical shapes and with classical architectural detail, was shown by firms such as J. and M. P. Bell of Glasgow, Ferguson and Miller, also of Glasgow, and Blanchard of Lambeth.

Classical shapes and classical decorative motifs became part of the general repertoire of ceramic ideas; but so far as directly imitative work was concerned the main influence of classical ideas was naturally on decorative earthenware or stoneware rather than on porcelain. In the 'fifties this museum-inspired interest tended to shift from classical Greek work to that of the Renaissance, and particularly of the French Renaissance. During the years following the 1851 Exhibition Mintons were producing their "Palissy ware", which was allied to their majolica of the same period and included pieces made in direct imitation of the work of the French sixteenth-century potter and his followers with high-relief decoration covered by coloured glazes. The elaborately inlaid Saint-Porchaire ware, normally known to the Victorians as "Henri Deux", was another French sixteenth-century source of inspiration for imitative work. The "Limoges ware" of Kerr and Binns, which attracted much attention at the Paris Exhibition of 1855, had little but a vague technical similarity with the Limoges enamels, but much of the distinctive white enamel painting was based on Renaissance arabesques and figure-work (Pl. 42A). It is noteworthy that versions of Palissy, Henri Deux and Limoges wares can all be found among the work of French factories of the period. Part of this French influence was undoubtedly due to the number of French artists who were employed in Staffordshire, and particularly by Mintons, during the 'fifties. Besides the art director Lèon Arnoux, Mintons employed a series of French sculptors primarily in modelling for majolica and parian work. During the 'fifties Emile Jeannest, Albert Carrier de Belleuse and Hugues Protat were employed in succession, and all of them were also instructors at the newly founded Potteries' Schools of Design.

Two other sources of inspiration need to be mentioned – the Gothic and the Moorish – which in the early Victorian context were largely architectural in origin. The use of Gothic patterns on stoneware jugs in the early 'forties has already been noted. In the middle 'forties Copelands were producing porcelain in a "pierced Gothic" pattern; and in the later part of the decade A. W. N. Pugin, the chief protagonist of the Gothic style, designed decorations for Mintons which were printed and painted on a number of tablewares in the Minton "New Stone" body and in porcelain, some of which were shown at the 1851 Exhibition. The Moorish decorations were used less frequently, but in a similar manner to the Gothic. They were most often known as "Alhambresque" and were derived from published illustrations of the stucco work in the Alhambra at Granada. They appear, for instance, on a jug and a flower-pot by Ridgway and Abington of Hanley which were illustrated in the *Art-Union* in 1845 and 1846: and at the Paris Exhibition of 1855 Copelands' chief exhibit was a three-feet-high Alhambresque vase which was said to be the largest vessel ever made of parian.

After the many imitative and derivative styles which have been mentioned, it is as well to point out that one of the most obvious sources of ceramic ideas, the pottery of the Far East, was largely ignored during this period. It was the period of reaction against the "Japan" patterns which had been prevalent earlier in the century and which in early Victorian times were only being produced at a low level of fashion. In a review of the work of the John Ridgway factory in the 1846 *Art-Union* a solitary vase in the "Chinese" style evokes the acid comment that it is "not of a class we desire to see multiplied". The Victorian revival of Far Eastern styles lay well beyond 1860. It should also be pointed out that whilst the modern eye is immediately struck by the elements of plagiarism in Victorian pottery and porcelain, it is rare to find that imitation has been so exact as not to leave scope for the expression of a contemporary Early Victorian spirit. Bemused as they were by the many examples of earlier work which were brought before their eyes, the early Victorian potters did nevertheless often combine these elements to produce work of original quality. Besides the free use of rococo and plant motifs, a number of distinctive styles emerged which were associated with particular factories. An example which has not so far been mentioned is the highly personal style of pierced porcelain made by Chamberlains of Worcester which attracted considerable interest in the years between 1846 and 1851 (Fig. 24). In general, the most publicized pieces tended to be the most imitative. Even around the middle of the century, when the Sèvres influence was at its strongest, Sèvres motifs appeared among the

Fig. 24. Stemmed bowl of pierced porcelain, made by Chamberlains of Worcester in the later 'forties. *Journal of Design and Manufactures* (11, 95).

everyday table-services as only one element among a vast range of patterns most of which were in their interpretation entirely characteristic of their own period.

Porcelain figures. The earthenware figures of the time have already been described as wares of a "peasant" quality. Porcelain figures were naturally more susceptible to fashion, and during this period came to diverge markedly from the earthenware figures not only in style but also in the nature of their conception. Some of the new porcelain figures of the years around the 'thirties, as seen particularly in the work of the Derby and Rockingham factories, were characterized by the use of strong contrasting colours applied flatly over large areas. The Derby biscuit figures were no longer made, apparently for technical reasons connected with the factory's organization of firings. A quantity of new porcelain figures, both glazed and painted and in biscuit, were being made at Mintons in the later 'thirties and in the 'forties, and some at least of these were in eighteenth-century costume.

A notable change of attitude towards porcelain figure-work came with the introduction of the parian porcelain body. This new body was used for many different purposes and for many different styles of hollow wares, but it was originally produced for making figures and it was for this purpose that it was considered ideally suitable. It is said that experiments were being made concurrently at both Copelands and Mintons towards the production of a material of this nature. At Copelands the parian body seems to have been produced in the course of attempts to rediscover with the help of an ex-employee of the Derby factory the formula of the old Derby biscuit body. The potentialities of the new body, and the manner in which it was mainly to be used, were expressed in the first group of parian figures from Copelands which were shown at the Manchester Exhibition of 1845–6. The same body, with slight variations, was soon being made by many factories. Copelands called it "statuary porcelain", Coalport and Wedgwoods called it "Carrara", but it was the Minton term "Parian" which eventually passed into the language. It was a comparatively hard form of porcelain, and as such was markedly different from the bone china which was otherwise in universal use as the standard British porcelain body. A writer in the 1846 *Art-Union* was already praising the "lustrous transparency" of the surface of the parian figures in comparison with the excess of reflected light in glazed figures and the complete lack of it in the older biscuit figures. Although not immediately apparent, parian was normally given a slight "smear" glaze, which imparted to it the dull smoothness of polished marble.

Modern taste is not easily reconciled to the use of one material in imitation of another. To the Early Victorians, who were inclined to emphasize imitative rather than original elements in the decorative arts, the resemblance of parian to marble justified the immediate and extensive use of the material for making figures in the style of marble statuary. The traditional rococo base, and the use of colour, suddenly became relatively unfashionable. Porcelain figures came to be called "statu-

F

ettes", and contemporary publicists were delighted at the elevating effect of copies of fine sculpture being within the reach of every home. The *Art-Union* of London prided itself upon its early recognition of the medium, and in 1846 commissioned reduced copies of John Gibson's "Narcissus" and J. H. Foley's "Innocence" (Pl. 41B) to be made by Copelands as prizes for its subscribers. In 1847 Mintons were producing two parian figures, both after John Bell, which were commissioned by Henry Cole for his "Summerly's Art Manufactures". Versions of Hiram Power's much-admired statue "The Greek Slave" appeared from 1849 onwards from Mintons, Copelands, and Pountneys of Bristol. R. J. Wyatt, William Theed junior (Pl. 41B), Carlo Marochetti, Richard Westmacott and W. Calder Marshall were among the other contemporary sculptors whose work was represented in parian. Many of the Copeland reductions from large-size statues were effected by the reducing machine of Benjamin Cheverton, and the name of Cheverton on the base of a figure has often been misinterpreted to imply that he was the modeller in the normal sense of the word. Statuary was not, however, the only source for derivative designs. A Minton group of about 1849 was taken from a picture of Ruth and Naomi by Henry O'Neil; and Mintons' Prince of Wales in a sailor-boy's costume, of about the same time, was an adaptation of Winterhalter's picture.

Following the example of the great dessert service made by Mintons for the 1851 Exhibition the use of parian figures in combination with normal glazed porcelain became a recognized mode for factory prestige work. Probably the most distinguished of this sort was the "Shakespeare service" made by Kerr and Binns for the Dublin Exhibition of 1853, in which Shakespearean figures, modelled by W. B. Kirk, were applied to porcelain pieces decorated with Renaissance motifs (Pl. 42B). Work of such virtuosity could not be considered typical, but the use of parian figures on great occasions was a measure of their popularity and of the extent to which the new medium was adapted to contemporary taste.

GLASS

TUDOR

AFTER the Saxon period there is a great gap in the knowledge of glass in England. It is certain, however, that by the thirteenth century glass was being manufactured here. This industry, situated in the well-wooded country of the Weald which supplied it with all the timber needed for its furnaces, was mainly devoted to the making of window-glass. The blowers, however, were certainly also capable of blowing simple vessels; and fragments of such vessels, of a thin green glass, have been found on the Wealden glass-house sites. Impure green glass of this sort, however, was probably restricted to humble domestic rôles, being made into lamps, bottles, urinals and the like. Glasses for table use were imported from abroad, mainly from Venice, the greatest glass-making centre in the world. Records of the glass used in England during the first half of the sixteenth century are in general not easy to find. But an ample existing inventory attests the considerable quantities of fine glass-ware owned by Henry VIII at the time of his death. His "Glasse Housse" at Westminster contained over six hundred pieces, the forms including bottles and flagons, basins and bowls with ewers, cups, cruses, spice-plates, candlesticks, and other less common shapes. These enviable chattels seem to have been made in most of the techniques known to the time. We read of "glasse iasper colloure", which must be the opaque glass coloured and streaked in imitation of natural stone and called by the Venetians "calcedonio"; of glass of many different colours, frequently "p[ar]tely guilte"; of glass with "white worke nette fashion", which must refer to the glass with elaborate decoration of crossing opaque-white threads called by the Venetians "vetro di trina" [or "lace-glass".] Along with the simpler items are described important pieces which must have served as centre-pieces for tables, or as "verres de parade" for sideboards – such as the "faire glasse the foote and cover garnished w[ith] silver and guilte upon the Toppe of the Cover A woman holdinge A skutchine in thone hande and A snake [?] in thother hande." Many of the glasses were, like this one, mounted in silver-gilt. One of these is referred to as "a glasse like a potte paynted and garnished aboute the brym[m]e w[ith] silver and guilte w[ith] a cover w[ith]out garnishinge". The use of the word "pot" probably implies a shape like that of the "maiolica" and stone-ware mugs already discussed, and there is in the British Museum a small mug of this form decorated with vertical stripes of white and mounted with a silver-gilt rim and cover which bear the date-mark for 1548 – one year after the preparation of this inventory (Pl. 45A). The use of the word "Paynted", however, as in the description of the "pot" just mentioned, is surprisingly rare, and this absence of references suggests that glasses with enamelled decoration had by this time gone out of fashion. At least one important enamelled Venetian glass, however, is known which has been in England ever since the sixteenth century (Pl. 44B). It was stated by the owner, when he bequeathed it in 1631 to the Founders' Company, to have formed part of the booty brought from Boulogne when it surrendered to Henry VIII in 1546. With this date the mark on the silver-gilt foot (a replacement) accords well enough.

Harrison, writing in 1577, says: "It is a world to see in these our days, where gold and silver most aboundeth, how that our gentility, as loathing those metals (because of the plenty) do now generally choose rather the Venice glasses, both for our wine [Pls. 44A, B, 46B] and beer, than any of those metals or stone wherein before time we have been accustomed to drink; ... and such is the estimation of this stuff that many become rich only with their new trade unto Murano (a town near to Venice, situate on the Adriatic Sea) from whence the very best are daily to be had. ... And as this is seen in the gentility, so in the wealthy commonalty the like desire of glass is not neglected, whereby the gain gotten by their purchase is yet much more increased to the benefit of the merchant. The poorest also will have glass if they may; but, sith the Venetian is somewhat too dear for them, they content themselves with such as are made at home of fern and burned stone ..."

This increase in the import of Venetian glasses was reflected in the formation of a Glaziers' Company, which received arms in 1588.

In the meantime, however, a far more important event had taken place. This was the start on English soil of glass-making in the Venetian manner. It began effectively probably in 1570, and was given official support by the grant in 1575 of an exclusive patent for the manufacture in England of Venetian-type glass. The patentee was one Jacob Verzelini, a Venetian who had migrated to this country by way of Antwerp. Roughly a dozen glasses can with reasonable probability be attributed to the period of Verzelini's monopoly (which was cut short in 1592), and of these all but three are decorated with diamond-point engraving. This technique (which covers the glass in fine spidery lines) was one widely used at the time on the thin glass of Venetian type. The English examples, however, are characterized by the division of the field of decoration (normally the bowl of a drinking-glass) into arabesques alternating with panels left plain, to be subsequently filled with the devices, initials or names of the persons ordering the glass, and frequently with the date (Pl. 44C). These range from 1577 to 1586. One glass, dated 1590, is decorated with similar devices and inscriptions, but the decoration is carried out in gilding instead of diamond-point engraving (Pl. 44A). Verzelini's monopoly was taken up after 1592, and only one English glass made between this date and 1603 is certainly known – the wine-glass in the Victoria and Albert Museum dated 1602 and inscribed with the name "Barbara Potter". In decoration, even if not in shape, it obviously belongs to the family of Verzelini's glasses. That this family should be decimated by time was only to be expected. It is nevertheless evident that by the end of Queen Elizabeth's reign glasses of this sort, many of them probably made in Verzelini's glass-houses at the Crutched Friars and in Broad Street, were common in the houses of the rich. Thus, in the residence of the Earl of Leicester at Kenilworth, in 1588, there were:

Ffyve plaine bole glasses, without covers.
Ffyve indented bole glasses, two graven bole glasses; twelve beare [beer] glasses of severall fashions,[1] iii with covers; two plaine taper glasses with covers; two other ribbed taper glasses; an embossed glasse with a cover; two glass ewers.

Glasse Dishes

Tenne glasse dishes gilte, with the sinque foyle on the brims.
Eight graven dishes of glasse aboute the brims.
Twelve greate standing indented bole glasses for creame.
A deep standing glasse, with a cover.
Ffyvteen glasses brode brimed and narrowe bottoms.
Ffowertene greate deepe glasses, viii of them plaine.
A dozen of dishe glasses of one sorte.
Two dozen and iiii dishe glasses of another sorte.

That these were of "Venice making", or the English surrogates, went without saying in a household of this pretension. In humbler homes, the possession of a piece of Venetian glass was worthy of special remark. Thus, in the inventory of a house at Cockesden, taken in 1610, occurs the entry: "In the Tapestrie Chamber" – "Item, there is the great Venise glasse..."

Venetian and Venetian-style glasses, however, were by no means the only, nor the commonest, glasses in use, as Harrison notes in the passage quoted above. The substitute glass was the humble green material made in the woodland glass-houses already referred to. The source of alkali in these forest houses was obtained by burning fern and other vegetable-matter and utilizing the lixiviated ashes. This was not so pure an alkali as the imported *barilla* (soda obtained from burned marine plants) used in Venetian glass-making; nor were the sources of silica so carefully selected, being often tainted with iron impurities which gave the glass a green tone. The resultant glossy green material nevertheless has æsthetic merits of its own, and the simple beakers, cups and bottles made in the English country glass-houses form a family which, although unpretentious, is well worthy of attention.

The impetus in the Wealden glass-manufacture during the Middle Ages had come from France, probably from Normandy and Poitou. In the middle of the sixteenth century, the same enterprising spirit which had established Venetian glass-making in London brought into the Sussex–Surrey industry an infusion of

[1] cf. Pl. 46A

Fig. 25. Reconstruction of a beaker with mould-blown design and thread-foot. Woodchester. Glos. *c.* 1600. Ht 4¾ in.

Fig. 26. Reconstruction of a beaker with threaded decoration. Woodchester, Glos. *c.* 1600. Ht 4½ in.

new blood – mainly from Lorraine, but also perhaps from the Flemish glass-houses. During the last quarter of the sixteenth century the country's dwindling resources of timber gave increasing concern, and the glass-makers of the forest-houses were forced – sometimes by actual shortage and sometimes by local hostility – to uproot themselves and settle wherever they could be assured of timber supplies. The wanderings of the Lorrainers from the Weald took them via Hampshire into the Border country and into Staffordshire, and the traces of their migration are to be found in church-registers, place-names and occasional glass-house sites. Most of these sites yield scanty information. At Woodchester, in Gloucestershire, however, excavation has provided fragments which enable us to form a clear picture of the work done in these forest-houses (whose staple, it should not be forgotten, was normally window-glass).

The glasses made at Woodchester fall into two main classes – drinking-glasses and bottles. The drinking-glasses were tall tumbler-like beakers of two types. The first kind were straight-sided and almost perfectly cylindrical, being made stable by the addition of a coil of glass round the foot and by the pushing-in of the base in a slight conical "kick" (Fig. 25). The second of the taller beaker-shapes was made by pushing in the bottom of the vesicle of glass whilst still soft, and thus making a low pedestal of double thickness, above which the body of the glass rose in the form of a slightly everted cylinder (Fig. 29). This method of fashioning the foot, which was characteristic of French glassmaking, was also used in making

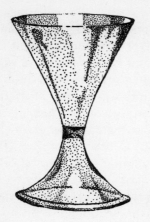  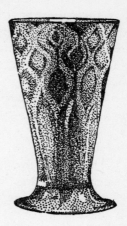

Fig. 27. Reconstruction of a wine-glass. Woodchester, Glos. *c.* 1600. Ht 5½ in.

Fig. 28. Reconstruction of a drinking-vessel in the form of a boot. Woodchester, Glos. *c.* 1600. Ht 4¾ in.

Fig. 29. Reconstruction of a beaker with mould-blown design. Woodchester, Glos. *c.* 1600. Ht 6 in.

goblets, the second main group of drinking-glasses. Here the pedestal base was constricted and extended to form a foot and "stem" (Fig. 27). Drinking-glasses were also made in the shape of a boot (Fig. 28) – a trick-form favoured in the Netherlands which survived in England until at least the eighteenth century.

The bottles made at Woodchester were quite small (the only intact example measures 5½ inches in height), and were normally hexagonal in section (Pl. 45B). One exceptional fragment, however, came from a flattened spherical bottle of German type, decorated with ribs blown in a mould and then "wrythen" to produce a diagonal patterning (cf. Pl. 45C).

Mould-blowing, indeed, was the most favoured method of decorating the glasses found on this site. The moulds imparted either a honeycomb pattern (Fig. 29) or a design of vertical ribs which could be twisted on withdrawal from the mould, to give the "wrythen" effect described above. Another favoured decoration was a trail of glass laid round and round the glass, either in a spiral (Fig. 26) or in a series of horizontal bands. In the latter case, the trails were sometimes combined with small applied blobs of glass stamped with a design like the pips of a raspberry. Similar "prunts" were worked, whilst still plastic, into the form of rosettes.

Of all the simple forms made, the beaker is by far the commonest, and there can be little doubt that these glasses were used by the commonalty for drinking beer. A writer at the end of the sixteenth century could say: "Take a Beer glasse of six or eight inches in height and being of one equal bigness from the bottome to the top", which admirably describes their general cylindrical form.[1]

[1] Sir Hugh Platt: *Jewell House of Art and Nature* (1st edn. 1594). London, 1653, p. 76.

Although the bottle fragments at Woodchester were not so numerous as those of beakers, there must have been in the late sixteenth and early seventeenth centuries a vast output of small green bottles for a variety of purposes (cf. Fig. 30). Small cylindrical phials, presumably used by apothecaries, are very commonly found in excavations in towns in this country, and are often mistaken for Roman glass. But fragments of bottles of square section or with globular bodies are also often found, and such convenient small receptacles must have had a number of uses. Thus, in an inventory of 1605, the following glass objects are noted (amongst others more easily identifiable): "2 glasses w[i]th Balsamum ...", "one big conserve glasses", "3 little Conserve glass, one hath sugar Candy", "4 little Conserve glass w[i]th oyles". These were almost certainly bottles of one sort or another (the word "glass" at this period meaning "bottle", as well as the modern "glass").

Bottles of larger capacity seem to have gone through a transitional phase at the end of the Tudor period and under the first Stuarts. At the beginning of the sixteenth century, they were probably mostly of imported Venetian glass, and had the common Venetian form of a spherical body mounted on a low foot, and surmounted by a longish slightly everted neck (Pl. 48B). At latest by the early seventeenth century it became customary to cover these thinnish bottles with leather or wickerwork for their protection: the inventory already referred to mentions "2 glasse bottles couerde w[i]th leather" and "one great wanded bottle of glasse". Such wickered bottles are almost invariably represented in seventeenth-century paintings as slightly flattened in the body, although it cannot at present be determined when the change from the spherical to the flattened body took place. So long as bottles were made of thin and fragile glass, the advantages of this shape were obvious. When, at a later date, bottles began to be made of stout green glass, they resumed the circular section – presumably for reasons of economy in making.

Of the many other domestic uses to which glass was put, lighting was undoubtedly one. Green glass fragments of what were certainly lamps are not infrequently found in the excavations of English cities, and probably date from the later Middle Ages. The form of these lamps was that of a cylindrical cup suddenly tapering below into a long point. This lamp was intended primarily for suspension. There is no evidence to show what sort of lamps were used in Tudor England, but that they could be of glass seems evident from an observation of Thomas Platter's in 1599. In Whitehall Palace he saw an emblem of "a glass full of oil and a light burning in it".

Finally, there was one use to which glass was put and for which it alone was suitable. This was for the making of urinals. The examination of urine was an essential element in the medical diagnosis of the period. William Vaughan in his *Naturall & Artificial Directions for health*, 1602, instructs his reader: "... in the morning make water in an vrinal: that by looking on it, you may ghesse some what of the state of your body..." In Henry VIII's possession at Westminster were "vii cases of wicker twoo of theym p[ar]telye guilte w[i]th vii brode mouthed Urynalls in theym w[i]th laces of thrid to eache of theym". This tradition continues and in the inventory of 1605 mentioned above there occurs the item: "one Ewrinall w[i]th the case hanging at thend [i.e. the end] of that Cupborde". Thus housed, it was no doubt readily available for use.

Fig. 30. An itinerant glass-seller of the mid-16th century, from a wood-cut.

STUART

DURING the sixteenth, and the greater part of the seventeenth centuries, European glass was dominated by Venice. The fine thin glass-metal (dubbed "cristallo", from its approximation to natural crystal in appearance), and the extraordinary dexterity of the Venetian workmen, combined to produce glasses of unrivalled elegance and fantasy. An English traveller writing in 1648 about Murano, the glass-making island close to Venice, says: "Here continually ... are Fornaces to make Glasses, which for the variety of the worke, and the Chrystall substance, exceed all others in the world, and are transported to all parts: out of which merchandise *Venice* drawes infinite summes of money." (See also p. 85). Potentates all over Europe tried to set up in their own dominions glass-houses working in the "façon de Venise", and many were successful, despite the fact that severe penalties were exacted by the Venetian state from any glass-worker who left Murano and revealed its secrets abroad. An account has been given in the last chapter of the setting-up in England of a glass-house manned by Italians and making glass of the Venetian kind. Glass nevertheless continued to be obtained from Venice sporadically throughout the seventeenth century, sometimes by special licence (as when, in 1619 and 1635, the import was otherwise specifically forbidden), sometimes through such agencies as were empowered to import it. It does not seem to have been in practice very difficult for anybody with influence in high places to get hold of Venetian glass. Such people would probably be more particularly anxious to obtain the highly-wrought goblets, with fantastic stems and finials, which were the delight of seventeenth-century glass-making. No doubt such a glass is referred to in the inventory taken at Marston Hall in 1605: "It. – one great knotted glasse *wth* a Couer called Charynge Crosse" (cf. Pl. 47A).

Glass-making in England during the first half of the seventeenth century was, like other industries, characterized by the system of monopolies. A somewhat confusing structure of privileges, apparently to some extent overlapping, was cleared away by an edict of 1615 which forbade the use of wood for firing glass-furnaces. The control of the glass industry was thereby effectively put in the hands of a combine which had at its disposal a successful method of coal-firing. This combine included among its members a certain Sir Robert Mansell, an Admiral and erst-

Bought of John Burroughs at the Glasse house without Ludgate London.

Fig. 31. A glass-maker at work in front of a glass furnace, in a possibly somewhat fanciful setting. From the bill-head (enlarged) of John Burroughs, Master of the Glass Sellers' Company, 1681–2.

while Treasurer of the Navy. After a tour of naval duty in the Mediterranean in
1620, Mansell successfully set about buying out the other members of the company, and in 1623 obtained from the King a new grant of letters patent to "use
exercise practise sett up and putt in use the arte feate and misterie of melting and
makeing of all manner of drinking glasses broade glasses windowe glasses looking
glasses and all other kinds of glasses, bugles bottles violls or vessels whatsoever
made of glass of any fashion stuff matter or metal whatsoever with sea cole pitt
coale or any other fewell whatsoever not being tymber or wood". This complete
control of the glass industry was exercised by Mansell until at least the period of
the Civil War, and during the Commonwealth the industry was still sufficiently
flourishing to be a fruitful source of revenue. Whether it remained so completely
under Mansell's control during this period, however, is uncertain, and Mansell
himself died four years before the Restoration of Charles II in 1660.

No glass certainly made in England between the accession of James I and the
end of the Commonwealth is known, but there are two sources of information
which throw light on the types made. The first is Mansell's own list of his products,
supporting a petition to the House of Lords, probably in 1639. From this it appears that he made principally wine-glasses and beer-glasses in three different
types of material – "ordinary" and two sorts of "cristall", of which one was somewhat more expensive than the other. Apart from these, he made "mortar-glasses"
(probably small bowl-like lamps), looking-glasses and "Spectacle-Glasse Plates",
window-glass and green glass of all sorts. The wine-glasses were no doubt in the
main stemmed forms, the beer-glasses being cylindrical beakers on a low pedestal
foot, of the type described and illustrated in the last chapter. We can fill in details
from the second source of our information concerning the glass-making of this
period – fragments excavated on English sites. These occur in considerable quantities, and often have a character which seems to mark them off from Venetian
products of the same period. In the first place, their metal is frequently somewhat
inferior, being rather thick and relatively lacking in translucency and lustre (these
may represent Mansell's second-quality "cristall"): in the second, their shapes and
decoration often diverge from the Venetian norm. The parts of wine-glasses most
frequently found, because most robust, are the stems, and of these (apart from the
normal Venetian type of pear-shaped stem moulded with lions' masks and
festoons) two patterns occur particularly frequently – those with a ladder-design
moulded on a pear-shaped stem, and those which are plain with a profile varying
from that of a fairly squat pear to that of a finely tapered "cigar". Occasionally a
stem occurs which shows the complex treatment of coiled threads or of applied
wrought "wings" familiar in the Netherlandish and Venetian glass-making of the
time. This decoration is referred to in the Mansell list as "of extraordinary
fashions". The English glass-houses of this period were still partly manned by
Italian workmen, some of whom are known to have been capable of this work.
The rather subdued character of this decoration may have been due either to

the sobriety of English taste, or to the modifying effect of English workmen's collaboration in their making. Wine-glasses, and cylindrical beer-glasses, are occasionally decorated by means of applied threads of opaque-white glass (a method also practised in the eighteenth century: see p. 100). The "ordinary Drinking-Glasses" of the 1639 list were no doubt of common green or greenish glass of the type made, for example, at the Woodchester glass-house and described in the previous chapter.

Fig. 32. Drawings for wine-glasses from amongst those sent by John Greene to accompany his orders for glass to Allesio Morelli in Venice, c. 1670. *British Museum.*

After the Restoration there was a return to a modified system of patents and monopolies, in which the Duke of Buckingham played a leading part, if only as a figurehead. For the first ten years of the period, however, imports of glass from Venice were permitted, and of greater significance than the monopolists in the evolution of glass in England were two new factors. The first of these was the rise of the Glass Sellers' Company, incorporated in 1664: the second was a gradual movement in European taste away from the light and fantastic qualities of Venetian glass towards a conception of glass as a surrogate of rock-crystal. The Glass Sellers' Company was a powerful and active organization, and by its position as intermediary between glass-house and customer, was able to influence the design of glass for the English market. Some of its members regularly obtained their supplies from Venice, and the orders of one of them, accompanied by detailed drawings, have fortunately been preserved, enabling us to form an idea of current taste in glass (Fig. 32; cf. Pl. 49A). These orders were sent by the firm of Measey and Greene to the house of Allesio Morelli at Murano, between 1667 and 1673. Minute instructions as to quantities and quality were given, and among these specifications occurs the significant phrase "verry Bright cleer and whit sound Mettall". This illustrates the second formative influence referred to above – the striving after a solid and clear glass resembling rock-crystal. In 1660 a Frenchman, John de la Cam, had signed an agreement with the Duke of Buckingham for the making of "Cristall de roach (cristal de roche) for and during the continuance of the Terme of Tenne yeares". The agreement did not run its full term, and in 1673 a more important project was set afoot, when a certain George Ravenscroft, who had been engaged in the Venetian trade, started a glass-house in the Savoy. Within a year Ravenscroft applied for a patent for "a particular sort of Christalline glass", and in 1674 he signed an agreement to supply glasses to the Glass Sellers' Company. This first type of glass suffered from a defect due to excess of alkali in the composition and known as "crizzling" – a proliferation of tiny gleaming hairlines in the body of the glass, often accompanied by a roughening of the surface. Ravenscroft, however, continued his experiments, probably under the ægis of the Glass Sellers' Company, and finally evolved a revolutionary new type of glass containing oxide of lead. This happened in about 1675, and the new metal was signalized by the use on vessels made from it of a seal impressed with a raven's head (from the Ravenscroft crest). At least seventeen such sealed vessels or fragments are known, and include bowls, bottles, jugs (cf. Pl. 47B), globular mugs, posset-pots, and wine-glasses of two forms.

The use of lead-oxide in glass spread throughout the "white" glass-houses in the country before the end of the seventeenth century, and the ratio of lead was continuously increased until, by about 1700, the metal took on a dark and "oily" brilliance. In Ravenscroft's glasses, and more markedly in the great covered goblets and posset-pots (Pl. 47A) of some ten years later, the traces of Italian workmanship are clearly to be seen, albeit modified to an anglicized idiom. Towards the close of the century, however, and particularly in wine-glasses, there emerged a style which was wholly English. This concentrated on the stem of the drinking-glass, in which it worked innumerable variations by different combinations of balusters and bulbs and flat discs. In all these a just proportion is observed between the bowl, the stem and the foot of a glass, and the sobriety and harmony of this style accord well with the taste of the "Queen Anne" epoch (Pls. 49B, 48C, 50B).

Apart from the "white" glass made for the table, green glass was made at a number of glass-houses up and down the country. Windows and wine-bottles formed the main produce of these houses, but, as already noted on p. 90, small globular and cylindrical bottles for apothecaries, and scientific and medical glasses of many sorts were also made. We have also noted that the typical wine-bottle of the late sixteenth and early seventeenth centuries had a flattened spherical form, and was usually of thin glass protected by a covering of wicker (Pl. 50A) or of leather. In an inventory of 1610 there occur under the heading "In the Buttery..." the entries: "Item, 4 leather bottles of glasse. Item, 2 wicker bottles, one of glasse" (cf. p. 90). Before the middle of the seventeenth century, however, a globular bottle of thicker and tougher glass had been evolved, perhaps originally for the storing of beer. In H. Platt's *Delightes for Ladies* (1644) occurs the passage: "When your Beere is ten or twelve dayes old, whereby it is growne reasonable cleere, then bottle it, making your corkes very fit for your bottles, and stop them close ..." By the middle of the century, bottles are mentioned which were tough enough to be sent by carrier and which contained wine: in 1651 Phineas Andrews, in Berkhamsted, Herts, sent to his friend Henry Oxenden, in Kent, "two doussen glasse bottles of the best Canary Dick Weeden hath". The earliest dated bottle bears a seal stamped 1657, and from now on we are able to follow accurately from dated and datable seals the evolution of the bottle shape (cf. Pl. 50B), right up to the appearance of the modern wine-bottle. Cork-screws are not known before 1686, and the binning of wine cannot have been practised much before this date. Mineral waters, however, were already being bottled, and Celia Fiennes in her *Journal* says of Tunbridge Wells (1697): "... they have the bottles filled and corked in the well under the water and so seale down the corke which they say preserves it ..."

In the seventeenth century, as in the one after, there was little distinction between the shapes of glasses used for different types of drink. Greene's drawings include stemmed types which could be used for beer as well as wine, and beaker shapes which could be used for wine as well as beer. The distinction, however, was rigorously observed at table. Shortly after the Civil War Lord Fairfax issued the following instructions to the servants of his household:

> The Cup-board.
> Let no man fill beere or wine, but the cup-board-keeper, who must make choice of his glasses or cups for the company, and not serve them hand over heade. He must also know which be for beer and which for wine; for it were a foule thing to mix them together.

Glasses were at this period kept on the cup-board, both for decoration and for use; in the latter case they were handed to the diners as called for, the glass being held by the foot (cf. Pl. 50A), and not by the bowl or stem. One exception to the indiscriminate use of glasses for different drinks seems to have been provided by the "romer" (German "Roemer"), a glass with a globular bowl, a wide, hollow stem decorated with applied patterned blobs of glass, and a conical foot. This glass, which was made in England (cf. Pl. 48A), was reserved for Rhenish wine; it is always seen in the Dutch still-life pictures of the seventeenth century. It is possible also that the tall tapering "flute" glass (Pl. 49C, cf. Pl. 50A) was used mainly, if not exclusively, for Spanish wines. Thus Richard Lovelace, writing in 1649, speaks of "Elles of Beare, Flutes of Canary".

GEORGIAN

ENGLISH glass in the eighteenth century took a course of its own which marked it out from that of the rest of Europe. The invention of lead-glass in 1675, referred to in the previous chapter, had resulted, by the end of the seventeenth century, in a heavy glass "metal" with a high degree of light-refraction. As already described, this was brought about by the increasing use of lead oxide in the composition. This glass, although brilliant, was often also dark in tone, probably as a result of excessive "de-colourizing". The new English "crystal" was both heavier in substance than the Venetian "cristallo" which had been the universal clear metal of seventeenth-century European glass-making, and took longer to cool while it was being worked. The light and fantastic touches which were both the effect and the inspiration of Venetian glass-making *legerdemain* were inappropriate to this more ponderous and glutinous substance. Although many tricks of Venetian ornamentation – frilled and pincered open-work stems and finials and the like – survived in the repertory of English glass-making, they were at first used only for elaborate "bespoke" work, and finally became entirely subordinated to the plain and monumental style in which lead-glass finally found its true soul. This was the period of the great "balusters", in the last years of the seventeenth and the opening years of the eighteenth centuries, when the thick, dark, yet brilliant, glass was ponderously wrought into goblet and wine-glasses with plain straight-sided bowls, deeply "folded" feet, and solid stems compiled of various knops and baluster-shaped elements.

"Wrought" stems. The monumental manner described above coincided roughly with the "Queen Anne" style in the decorative arts, and was succeeded by a phase in which lighter forms were favoured, and the severity of the balusters gave way before a greater variety of bowl-forms and combinations of stem-elements (Pls. 51C, 52A, 52D; 54C). The straight-sided bowl acquired a graceful out-curved profile or became bell-shaped, whilst a technique of drawing both bowl and stem from one piece of glass resulted in one of the most beautiful forms of glass ever made in this country – the "drawn-stem" glass, with its taut continuous curving profile (Pl. 53A). In many instances this "drawn" element was set above an inverted baluster

(Pl. 51C) to produce another very satisfying glass-shape. The "drawn stem", however, had been already in use in the glass-making of the *façon de Venise*, and the chief innovation in English glass-production in the early part of the period under review was the "pedestal" or "Silesian" stem. This appears to have originated in the German sphere of glass-making (although the term "Silesian" is almost certainly a misnomer), and in its earliest form occurs as a four-sided shouldered pedestal. Examples are known which have moulded on the four sides the words GOD SAVE KING G (Pl. 52C), and although the German influence represented by this stem is more probably to be attributed to the prestige of German glass, and to its large-scale irruption on to the European market after the Treaty of Utrecht (1713), these simple forms of the "Silesian" stem do probably date from the accession of our first Hanoverian King, or immediately afterwards. From the quadrilateral stem evolved polygonal types, often with ribs at the angles (and sometimes a boss surmounting each rib), the original design being imparted by pressing in a mould, and the stem being thereafter drawn out to the length and thickness desired. The stem-section so formed could be either welded directly to the base of the bowl, or could be separated from it by a knop and one or more discs of glass. Towards the middle of the century this stem-form began to fall out of use for wine-glasses and to be taken up in other forms, notably candlesticks (Pl. 51D), sweetmeats and dessert-salvers. In the last-named it continued well into the second half of the century, degenerating somewhat in sharpness of form, the ribs being often slightly twisted into a spiral.

The pedestal stems and the lighter types of baluster stems (sometimes called "balustroids") held the field during the third and fourth decades of the century, but in 1745–6 a fiscal measure was introduced which militated against the use of more metal in a glass than was absolutely necessary. This was the glass excise, which levied a tax on glass-material *by weight*. It has sometimes been assumed that this alone brought about a change in English glass-style, causing the glass-makers to abandon the plastically conceived stem as the main ornamental feature of a glass, and to concentrate on other forms of decoration applied to a glass with a plain stem. It is more likely, however, that the glass excise merely gave a final impetus to a movement in taste which was already taking place. During the decade before the middle of the eighteenth century the baroque style was giving way to the rococo, in which lightness of form and relatively superficial decoration played an all-important part. In the case of drinking-glasses, decoration first manifested itself in the stem.

Air- and enamel-twist stems. As early as the beginning of the seventeenth century English glass-makers had been wont to decorate glasses by means of moulded ribbing drawn out and simultaneously twisted, thus producing a close spiral (see p. 89). In the early decades of the eighteenth century there are isolated examples of *air-bubbles* within a glass being similarly drawn out and twisted to

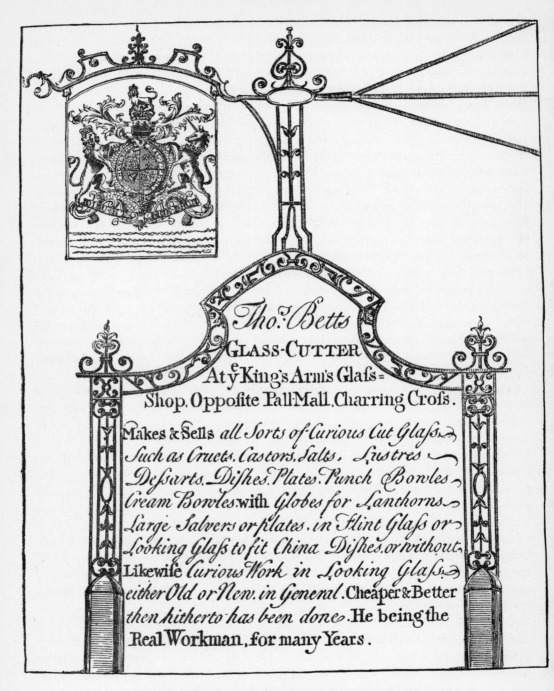

Tho.ˢ Betts
GLASS-CUTTER
At yᵉ King's Arm's Glaſs=
Shop, Oppoſite Pall Mall, Charring Croſs.

Makes & Sells all Sorts of Curious Cut Glaſs,
Such as Cruets. Castors. Salts. Lustres
Deſſarts. Diſhes. Plates. Punch Bowles
Cream Bowles with Globes for Lanthorns
Large Salvers or plates. in Flint Glaſs or
Looking Glaſs to fit China Diſhes. or without.
Likewiſe Curious Work in Looking Glaſs,
either Old or New. in General. Cheaper & Better
then hitherto has been done. He being the
Real Workman, for many Years.

Fig. 33. Trade card of Thomas Betts, London, about 1740-50.

produce an internal cable of thin air-lines: but the full development of this decoration for drinking-glasses seems to set in during the 1730's (cf. Pl. 56c). It probably suggested itself first in the "drawn-stem" glasses, which had frequently been decorated with an air-bubble trapped at the base of the bowl, and which by the nature of their manufacture, lent themselves to this drawing and twisting process. With increasing proficiency, however, the glass-maker was able to extend the use of air-twists to stems with one or more baluster-like swellings (Pl. 53B, D). Somewhat before the middle of the century the columns of air trapped within the stem were occasionally replaced by rods of opaque-white (or "enamel") glass, these rods being stood in a circular mould and "picked up" on a blob of glass in which they were then incorporated, the whole being drawn out and twisted as before. Occasionally, air-twists were used in conjunction with enamel-twists, and sometimes the white enamel canes were replaced by canes of coloured transparent or opaque glass. The "enamel", "mixed" and "coloured" twists were usually made in lengths which could be cut up and used to make a number of straight stems (Pls. 52B, 56A, 57B). The heyday of enamel twists was the third quarter of the century; a further excise in 1777, which extended the tax to enamel-glass, giving the death-blow to what was already probably a dying fashion.

All these decorative techniques were practised in the glass-house and were intrinsic to the glasses themselves. They were carried out while the material was still hot and ductile. During the period under consideration, however, a number of other methods of ornamentation came into vogue. Without exception, their technical origins may be sought in Germany, from which country both workmen and ideas reached England under the favourable conditions provided by the settlement of 1713 and the presence on the English throne of a German sovereign.

Engraved and cut glasses. Of these imported techniques, two are closely related. Both consist of grinding away the surface of the glass by means of a rapidly revolving wheel on to which is fed a stream of abrasive suspended in a liquid. In the first (engraving) the small copper wheels vary in profile and can be rapidly interchanged in the chuck of the power-shaft to suit the needs of the work in hand; in the second (cutting) the wheels, of iron or stone, are large, and in the eighteenth century were somewhat blunt of profile, either flat, rounded or mitred. A skilful engraver can render intricate devices or delicately modelled forms of great fineness, whilst the cutter grinds away planes and surfaces in such a way as to enhance the play of light and multiply images in his transparent medium. In Germany and Bohemia the seventeenth century produced complete masters of both techniques, and at the accession of George I, German prestige in this art was supreme.

Glasses with inscriptions and coats-of-arms engraved in the manner described above are known from the reign of Queen Anne, but they are rare, and the circumstances in which they were engraved are unknown. The engraving of such armorial or propaganda glasses to order continues through the first half of the

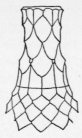

Fig. 34. Neck of a decanter showing fluting, scale-pattern and flat diamonds, about 1760–70 (after Thorpe).

Fig. 36. Field of strawberry diamonds, early nineteenth century (after Thorpe).

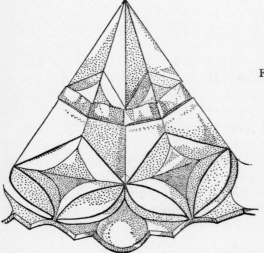

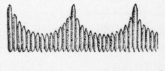

Fig. 37. "Herring-bone" fringe, early nineteenth century (after Thorpe).

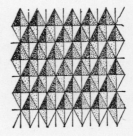

Fig. 35. Section of a dish showing the full development of English sliced cutting, about 1775.

Fig. 38. Field of relief diamonds, late eighteenth and early nineteenth centuries (after Thorpe).

eighteenth century (Pl. 56c), but is supplemented (probably from the 1720's onwards) by the use of decorative borders which, in their technical competence and in their display of characteristic German baroque ornamental motifs, reveal the hand of the immigrant artist. This border-style is transformed by the middle of the eighteenth century, the neat formality of the ornament being replaced by freer and less coherent designs of scrolls and leaves and flowers (Pl. 53A). These betray an English taste, if not necessarily an English hand, although English engravers were certainly at work by then. Well before the middle of the century, too, these same flowers and leaves had strayed from the borders to occupy the bowl of the glass. Amongst these "flower'd" glasses are to be found the not uncommon wine-glasses, engraved with Jacobite symbols, beloved by the treasonable societies of the mid-eighteenth century, and by the glass-collector of today (Pl. 53D). Figural engraving is not common on English glass, but occasionally renders pleasantly the *chinoiseries* of the French engravers of decorative prints; or the more English land-scapes with ruins, or vignettes of country life, as we know them on contemporary porcelain. This work belongs mainly to the 1760's and 1770's, and, in all of it, German correctness and refinement were modified to suit the less formal and exacting, and often more bucolic, taste of the English gentleman (Pls. 51B; 53A, B; 56D).

Glass-cutting had a similar early history in England, but was far more signifi-cant than engraving for the future development of English glass.

It succeeded for two reasons: firstly, because cutting was a decorative tech-nique intimately related to the form of the vessel on which it was used, and secondly, because English lead-glass was ideally suited to it, both because it was soft and therefore easily worked, and because its high refractive index brought out the maximum play of light. In the main, it was a German technique grafted on to the indigenous art of the plate- and mirror-grinders, who had already flourished in England in the seventeenth century. In the second decade of the eighteenth century, cut sconces were being advertised in London, and a German craftsman, John Akerman, had already settled there. As early as 1722 a Scottish visitor remarked on "a high scaloped glass" seen during the dessert-course at a fashionable dinner; in 1728 the same visitor observed sweetmeat glasses with "cornered brims". This early cutting was restricted when possible to the thickest and most easily accessible parts of a glass. Thus the edge of a sweetmeat glass might safely be notched into a scalloped or serrated border, while its stem could be cut into flat vertical flutes or alternating hexagonal facets (Pl. 51A, cf. Fig. 34). On the thinner parts of a glass the cut motifs were at first shallower and more hesitant (Pl. 53C). By the middle of the century, however, the skill of the cutter had ripened to a point where he could cover the whole of a vessel with cut motifs, including asymmetrical lunate "slices" formed by presenting the glass at an angle to the cutting-wheel; diamonds in low relief; and scalloped edges of far greater complexity than hitherto (Fig. 35).

When the neo-classical movement began to make itself felt in glass, it had the effect of sobering down the rich cutting-style of the 1760's and 1770's. Amongst the cut motifs which remained in favour, however, were the vertical flute, with its elegant slimming effect, and the relief-diamond.

The course of development of cut-glass was affected within a very short span of years by the impact of two economic measures. The first of these was the severe increase in 1777 of the tax on glass by weight: the second was the freeing of Irish trade in 1780. Ireland was now free to export glass anywhere in the world, and her glass-makers were unhampered by the Excise. The effects were twofold. In the first place, many English glassmen migrated to Ireland: in the second, the development of style in cutting was unhampered in Ireland by considerations of economy. It was therefore naturally the Irish glass-houses which took up and developed those motifs which required the greatest thickness of metal – the pillared flute (in relief), the deep horizontal groove, and, most important, the relief-diamond (latterly made smaller and shaiper), with its developments, the hob-nail diamond and the strawberry diamond. These, arranged overall in relatively large fields, and often combined with fluting, became the dominant motifs of late eighteenth- and early nineteenth-century cutting (Figs. 36–8). Their uniformity called for great precision in cutting, but led to aesthetic monotony and a boring profusion of decoration, seen at its worst towards 1850.

Coloured, enamelled and gilt glass. The glass-makers of the early eighteenth century, confident of the superiority of their own glass-material, seem to have scorned the use of metallic oxides to colour it. Already by about 1725 or 1730, however, green and blue glasses with air-twists and engraved borders were being made, and to these colours was added in 1754 a ruby-red invented by a German immigrant named Mayer Opnaim. Probably also of German origin was the practice of enamelling on glass, which appears to have begun in England about the middle of the eighteenth century. The spirit of Bewick's tail-pieces, with their vignettes of English rural life and scenery, informs some of the best enamelling of the period. Nor is this altogether surprising, for Bewick himself was apprenticed in the family which was responsible for the best of it. This was the Beilby family at Newcastle-on-Tyne, of whom William and Mary were entrusted with the work on glass. The best of their enamelling is done in monochrome white on drinking-glasses and decanters, although their ambitious armorial goblets in full heraldic colours are splendid things. Their simpler pieces are decorated with no more than a scroll of the fruiting vine or a flower-spray, but on the more elaborate glasses appear little vignettes of rural life and sport (Pl. 56A), classical ruins and obelisks in the taste of the time, or fictitious coats-of-arms painted in colours but enclosed in the most delicate of rococo scrollwork painted in white.

Although, later in the century, colourless glass was decorated by means of enamelling, the art was most commonly practised on opaque-white glass. This material was already known to English glass-makers in the seventeenth century (see p. 95), and, after a brief eclipse in the early eighteenth century, seems to have come into its own again about 1730. From then until about 1770 there was a continuous production of decorative vessels (jars and beakers for garnitures, candlesticks, mugs, salt-cellars, etc.) often decorated in fine enamel-colours (Pl. 54B). The heyday of this painting seems to have been about 1755–65, and it clearly coincides with the rage for porcelain enamelled on a white ground which obtained at this time. The ornamentation simulated that of porcelain, mainly in sprays and sprigs of flowers, often accompanied by the little insects first familiarized on European porcelain by the factory at Meissen. Contrary to popular belief, the opaque-white glass was not made only, or even mainly, in Bristol; but also in

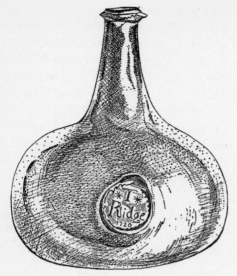

Fig. 39. Bottle of blackish-green glass, with seal impressed "T. Ridge, 1720". Ht 7⅛ in. *Victoria and Albert Museum*.

Fig. 40. Blue glass finger-bowl with gilt decoration. Signed "I. Jacobs Bristol". Probably made at Jacobs' "Non-Such Flint Glass Manufactory" in Bristol, about 1805. Ht. 3⅞ in. *Victoria and Albert Museum*.

London, Newcastle, Warrington and elsewhere. Some of it was almost certainly decorated in the South Staffordshire area, in which enamelling on metal had been practised since well before the middle of the eighteenth century. Here, too, were probably decorated the small faceted scent- and smelling-bottles, *étuis*, etc., of blue, green or purple glass, with their tiny scenes of birds, flying and swimming, or their inch-high shepherdesses with hay-rakes. These were usually enamelled and gilt, but sometimes gilt only, and this type of decoration became popular on blue glass in the same period which saw the "mazarine blue" grounds on Chelsea porcelain decorated with birds in thick rich gold. The bases of candelabra were often decorated in this way, while some blue fingerbowls and stands with gilt key-fret borders are among the few examples of glass certainly attributable to Bristol, being signed by the maker (Fig. 40). Such finger-bowls, however, must have enjoyed a general vogue at the time, for a German visitor remarks: "The blue glass bowls used for rinsing hands and mouth in at the end are quite delightful" (1786). Smollett, however, writing in his *Travels* (1766), thought quite differently about this habit: "I know of no custom more beastly than that of using water-glasses in which polite company spirt and squirt and spue the filthy scourings of their gums." Colourless glass, too, was occasionally decorated with gilding. This work is usually unpretentious, and consists of no more than a stem of vine-leaves and grapes, or the like.

The uses of glass. Glass in this period was used in almost as many ways as it is today. Then as now, however, glass for drinking took pride of place, and among drinking-glasses the wine-glass was king (Pls. 56B, C; 57A, B). On it and its concomitant decanter were lavished the most up-to-date forms of decoration. There was not, however, with one or two insignificant exceptions, a differentiation between the shapes and sizes of glasses used for different types of wine. This was a product of nineteenth-century connoisseurship. The wine-glass was simply a glass of about one-third to one-half gill in capacity, of varying bowl-shape. Somewhat smaller than the wine-glasses, but often on a proportionately higher stem, was the glass used for drams or cordials (Pl. 56A) – and small wonder, when one reads some of the recipes of the time:

A very rich Cherry Cordial.

"Take a Stone Pot that has a Broad Bottom and a narrow Top, and lay a layer of Black Cherries and a Layer of very fine powdered Sugar; do this 'till your pot is full: Measure your Pot and to every Gallon it holds, put a quarter of a pint of Spirit of Wine. You are to pick your Cherries clean from Soil and Stalks, but not wash them. When you have thus filled your Pot, stop it with a Cork, and tie first a Bladder, then a Leather over it; and if you fear it is not close enough, pitch it down close and bury it deep in the Earth six months or longer; then strain it out and keep it close stopped for your Use. 'Twill revive, when all other cordials fail."

A further type of glass of small capacity, with a tallish narrow bowl, is usually termed a "ratafia" glass, but ratafia was little different from other cordials, and a good case has been made out for these glasses being in fact champagne-glasses. Champagne, then as now, was an expensive drink (in 1762 it was offered at 8*s.* a bottle, as contrasted with 6*s.* for Burgundy or 5*s.* for Claret), and was apparently notable for its strength. Lady Mary Wortley Montagu, somewhat earlier, wrote:

They sigh not from their hearts, but from their brain
Vapours of vanity and strong Champaign.

That the champagne-glass offered one of the exceptions to the rule of non-differentiation enunciated above is proved by the fact that, in bills rendered by the glass-cutter, Thomas Betts, in the 1750's, "champagnes" are singled out by contrast with mere "wines". There is good reason why these champagne-glasses should have been small, and the almost cylindrical shape is, from the wine-taster's point of view, better for champagne-drinking than the modern shallow hemisphere – a form which probably did not come in before the second quarter of the nineteenth century. The eighteenth-century glasses of this general shape are certainly almost always sweetmeat-glasses.

Set apart from the form of the ordinary wine-glass was the "firing-glass" or the toast-master's glass. The latter might be a trumpet-shaped glass on a slender stem, or a glass with a deceptive capacity obtained by the use of abnormally thick metal. The "firing-glass" was usually trumpet-shaped, short-stemmed, and equipped with a thick disc-foot able to withstand hard banging on the table, in an age when drinking was of the order described in Dyott's *Diary*: "The Prince (afterwards

George IV) took the chair himself and ordered me to be his Vice. We had a very good dinner and he sent wine of his own, the very best Claret I ever tasted. We had the Grenadiers drawn up in front of the messroom windows to fire a volley in honour of the toasts. As soon as dinner was over he began. He did not drink himself: he always drinks Madeira. He took very good care to see everybody fill, and he gave 23 bumpers without a halt. In the course of my experience I never saw such fair drinking. When he had finished his list of bumpers, I begged leave as Vice to give the Superior, and recommended it to the Society to stand up on our chairs with three times three, taking their time from the Vice. I think it was the most laughable sight I ever beheld to see our Governor, our General and the Commodore all so drunk they could scarce stand on the floor, hoisted up on their chairs with each a bumper in his hand; and the three times three cheers was what they were afraid to attempt for fear of falling . . . There were twenty dined; we drank sixty-three bottles of wine."

Ale was drunk from glasses with tall tapering bowls. In high-class specimens, the bowl is frequently decorated with a hops-and-barley motif engraved, enamelled or gilt (Pl. 57c). In taverns, the glasses were plain, or at best ornamented with a wrythen mould-blown rib-pattern.

Tumblers were used for drinking strong drinks perhaps more frequently than is generally realized, and in 1717 Lord Cardigan laid in a stock of three dozen of them. Punch-bowls (Pl. 51B) and monteiths (wine-glass coolers with notched edges from which the glasses hung down in water) were also occasionally made in glass.

The decanter of the early part of the period followed roughly the form of the plain green-glass bottle (cf. Pl. 54A and Fig. 39). About the middle of the century, however, two new forms evolved. The first (Pl. 56D) again followed the form of the sloping straight-sided glass bottle of the period, and was frequently decorated by engraving, enamelling or gilding (often with a cartouche enclosing the name of the wine); the second was a shouldered form, broader at the top than lower down (Pl. 57D), and was usually decorated with all-over diamond-cutting. Decanters could vary in capacity from a pint (which must surely have stood at one man's elbow and not been passed round the table) to the equivalent of twenty bottles. The wine-glasses which they accompanied, and which were often *en suite* with them, were decorated in similar fashion. With the coming of neo-classicism these decanters were refined by a reduction in diameter and by a smooth unbroken transition in the curve from the neck to the body. These elegant decanters were usually only lightly decorated. From 1775 onwards an entirely new form takes the field – a decanter with barrel-shaped body and outsplayed lip. This shape was well-suited for decoration by cutting, and was taken over by the Irish glass-houses. Towards the end of our period the disc-stopper was replaced by a mushroom-stopper, and the neck of the decanter was equipped with three horizontal rings to facilitate a grip (Fig. 41).

Spirits, too, were kept in decanters, frequently of coloured glass with gilt labels showing their contents. These were often square in section and could, therefore, easily be carried about in travelling-cases. Thus in 1784 Fogg & Son, the noted London "chinamen" and glass-sellers, supplied Sir John Griffin with "4 Square Glass Bottles Cut All Over – 10/-". Such bottles were often simply referred to as "Squares".

Although the service of alcohol was the most important function of glass in the eighteenth century, its use spread far beyond this. At table, cruet-bottles and sugar-casters were frequently made of glass fitted with silver mounts, and when the dessert-course came on, glass had a particularly important part to play, for the centre of the table was frequently taken by an imposing "pyramid" of glass. A broad salver on a low foot formed the bottom tier of this pyramid, and on it was set another of narrower diameter but with a taller stem: and on this sometimes a third. Each tier was set round with jellies (Fig. 42) or wet and dry sweetmeats, in tall conical or low round glasses, whilst as the crown of the whole was set a large sweetmeat glass with hemispherical bowl on a tall stem (Pl. 55, cf. Pl. 51A), often containing preserved fruit and sometimes therefore called the "orange" (or "top") glass. Dishes, plates and pickle-trays of scalloped and sliced cutting might also adorn the table, whilst openwork baskets wrought from glass-threads whilst still plastic might serve to hold fruit. Tea-caddies, and more rarely teapots and cups and saucers; jugs and basins, patch-boxes, *étuis* and seals, were also occasionally made in glass.

Fig. 41. Decanter and stopper, cut with panels of "strawberry diamonds". Early nineteenth century. Ht 9⅛ in.

Of all the uses to which English glass was put in the eighteenth century none was more suited to its peculiar character than its employment for lighting fittings. The high powers of light-refraction possessed by English lead-crystal have already been mentioned: when cut, a prismatic effect was added to it, and when wax candles were set in cut chandeliers and candelabra, the effect must have been brilliant indeed – but of a brilliance softened by the slight darkness of the glass-material itself. The candlesticks of our period were mostly plain-shafted, with a broad domed foot and a detachable grease-pan. The shaft was usually cut in diamond facets, the foot and grease-pan scalloped and cut in accordance with the changing modes of the time.

Far more elaborate were the great cut-glass chandeliers which blazed in the reception rooms of great houses, or in the Assembly rooms of such cities as Bath, York or Newcastle. The glass chandelier had evolved in the first half of the eighteenth century to a form where S-shaped arms radiated from a semi-spherical cup which was itself only one of a number of spherical ornaments, usually simply cut, strung on a tall vertical shaft. In the second half of the century this basic pattern was merely elaborated. To the shaft were added canopies, scalloped at the edges and pierced for hanging drops cut in a variety of patterns; cutting became more elaborate, the candle-arms themselves being notched to add to the prismatic effect, and cut spires, themselves often topped by cut canopies, being set on the branches (Pl. 58). This was the apogee of the rococo chandelier. The first effects of neo-classicism were to be seen in the appearance of an urn-shaped member on the vertical stem, and gradually the whole chandelier began to be stripped of its more frivolous trappings. Cutting became sparser, and the medley of hanging ornaments gave way to a uniform type of brilliant-cut, usually pear-shaped, drop. These drops were often strung in swags from branch to branch and round the canopies, and the multiplication of these festoons of drops began to obscure the basic design of the chandelier. Arms, no longer readily visible, became plain, while the ornamental parts of the stem, except the canopies, lost importance. The final stage of this evolutionary process, which culminated about 1810, saw the eighteenth-century chandelier completely transformed. Below a series of drop-hung canopies, ropes of drops formed a sparkling tent, the widest part of which was an ormolu hoop, in which were set numerous short, S-shaped arms, heavily notched and terminating in richly cut candle-holders and grease-pans (Pl. 58).

The chandelier, which must have formed so striking an adjunct of the eighteenth century salon, was not, however, without its disadvantages. Lady Mary Coke, writing in 1768, remarks: ". . . I went to the Ball at eight o'clock . . . I think 'tis one of the finest Houses for an entertainment that I know, and nobody does the honours better or more agreeably than Lady Holland, yet I cant say I thought it went off well. The Dancers complained of the heat . . . A great branch Candle Stick fell down over Lady Holland, and very narrowly missed her head."

Common glass. The glass so far described was, for the most part, of a luxurious character, and reserved to the houses of wealth and importance. It was made in glass-houses devoted solely to the manufacture of "white" glass. Far more numerous, however, especially in the Bristol, Stourbridge and Newcastle areas, were the window- and bottle-houses. In the latter, enormous quantities of bottles were produced by hand, whilst in their spare time, using the fag-end of a pot of "metal", the workmen might produce simple jugs, cream-pans and the like, to satisfy a local market (Fig. 43).

The wine-bottle in the reigns of the first two Georges evolved from a low, onion-shaped flask (Fig. 39), through a phase corresponding to the "slope-shouldered" decanter (Pl. 56D), to a cylindrical form which was in all essentials that of the modern wine-bottle. This could be binned on its side to obviate "corking", instead of being stored neck down, as was sometimes done with the "onion"-shaped bottles. The eighteenth-century bottle was blown by hand and not moulded, and still bore round its neck the ribbon of glass which had originally served as an anchor for the wire fastenings of the cork. Occasionally a bottle is equipped with a seal bearing the name or arms of the owner of a cellar, or of a vintner or a College Common Room. Apart from wine- and beer-bottles, bottles were made for pickles and mustard, and (as in the seventeenth century and earlier) cylindrical phials for apothecaries' use. Spa waters could still be obtained bottled (see p. 97), and although those of Pyrmont and Pouhon were probably put up in the bottles of the Spa in question, others were certainly English. Thus, "Alexander Douglas Chymist at Glauber's Head near St. Clement's Church" sold "Spaw and Pyrmont Waters, Right French Hungary Water, ... Daffy's Elixir, Stoughton's Drops, &c." These last were probably put up in small mould-blown phials with the contents noted in relief lettering on the outside. Somewhat later in the century a glass-house at Dudley advertised a stock of "43 gross Lavender's, Daffy's, Turlington's and Smith's Bottles"; many surviving examples of such relief-moulded

Fig. 42. Jelly-glass. Mid-eighteenth century. Ht 4½ in.

Fig. 43. Green glass jug decorated with blobs and threads of opaque-white glass. Late eighteenth or early nineteenth century. Ht 7¾ in.

phials for Turlington's "Balsam of Life" are known. From such a bottle one may
picture Sylas Neville taking his daily dose in 1767: "Read an account of some of
the cures performed by the "Baume de Vie" since its publication here. I wish mine
was added to the number. I take about 3 small table-spoonfulls every day."

The standard wine-bottle of this period contained a quart, although hand-
making rendered it difficult to maintain exact uniformity – so much so that a
Member of Parliament, suitably enough the Member for Cork, brought in a
Private Member's Bill in 1802 "that a quart bottle should hold a quart". There
were, however, also half-bottles, and even quarter-bottles; while, on the opposite
side of the scale, there were Jeroboams and Rehoboams accommodating 4 and 6
bottles respectively, Methuselahs for 8 and Salmanazars for 12, and even monsters
which held 28 bottles.

REGENCY

Glass. Flint-glass was never more splendid than in the days of the Regency and George IV. Lavish cutting gave it a spectacular prismatic fire, as innumerable diamond shapes were cut deeply and expertly over the entire surface of table ware or ornament. But equally notable in its way was this period's accomplishment in providing a reasonably effective substitute for this craftsman-created glitter, so that middle-class homes could enjoy less costly decorative glassware shaped by blowing in open-and-shut moulds and only finished by hand. Glass-cutters from about 1810 were installing steam-driven cutting wheels, the speed of production enabling more complex patterns to be cut at no extra cost. The high excise duty, however, ensured that finely cut flint-glass remained in the luxury class of domestic refinements. The size of the diamonds was gradually lessened, the tendency being to reduce cross-cut diamonds to small plain diamonds and the latter to even smaller dimensions from about 1820, when prismatic- or step-cutting was also used with scintillating effect.

Armorial table services were a source of pride to those who could afford them at this period. A combined wine and dessert service would consist of more than five hundred matching pieces, blown from the finest piling pot glass and each engraved with an expansive coat of arms cut on a shield against a plain ground reserved in the cutting design. Some of these coats of arms were superb examples of the glass engraver's craft, the Lambton arms, for instance, possessing a shield with twenty-five quarterings. The Marquess of Londonderry's service made by the Wear Flint Glass Company in 1824 cost two thousand guineas. This was designed for twenty-four covers and consisted of more than five hundred pieces, including wine-glasses in four sizes, ship's decanters and other quart-size decanters, claret jugs, water jugs (Pl. 60B), finger bowls, wine-glass coolers, tumblers, dry sweetmeat jars (Pl. 61A), dessert dishes and plates.

The shapes of table ware during the period were based on geometric forms. Decanters, for instance, were cylindrical, at first with deep relief cutting on the shoulders and from 1820 with prismatic cutting, and by the mid-1820's with horizontal shoulders. These vessels were of thick section and much heavier to lift than formerly. The body was fashionably encircled with two or three bands of

112

contrasting cut motifs separated by flat polished rings. These were produced in endless variations. Some of the most complex designs in diamond-cutting are to be found on cylindrical decanters from about 1820. Mushroom stoppers continued in use until about 1820 when heavy pinnacles became the fashionable stopper finials. Mouths flared widely and gracefully outward from immediately above the neck rings. At the coronation of William IV in 1831 Apsley Pellat introduced the "royal shape" nearly cylindrical decanter with sides slanting outward from the shoulder to base and these cut with twelve or fourteen bold vertical flutes. Fancy decanters date from the same year.

The fashion for drinking hot toddy increased during the late Regency years, and many a home possessed a pair of giant rummers in which the toddy was prepared. A bucket or ovoid (Pl. 59B) bowl was usual on such a rummer, and this might be lavishly engraved with personal emblems or cut in a stock pattern with a cartouche left for engraving crest or cypher. Such a rummer was accompanied by a toddy lifter – a pipette with a long slender tubular neck terminating in a bulbous container, drilled with a hole in its flat base. Among other glassware that now found a place in the home were such pieces as beehives and covers for honey, butter boats with handles, and egg-cups.

Table glass might be blown within a two-piece open-and-shut mould which had come into general use by 1810. By this means the form of the vessel and elaborate all-over designs in relief could be made in a few simple hand operations. By 1820 three-piece moulds were in use. This process brought flint-glass to the everyday tables of the middle-classes and into general use on formal occasions among the not-so-rich.

Almost every vessel made by free-blowing and hand-cutting was reproduced in the open-and-shut mould, such as celery vases, sugar basins, *compote* bowls, salt cellars, hats for tooth-picks, jugs, casters. Some hollow-ware vessels, such as cordial decanters, salad bowls, rummers and so on, were given pinched square feet, made separately and welded into position. Until the early 1820's the patterns on blown-moulded glass were geometrical; then baroque ornament was made possible by the three-piece mould and designs included fanciful curves in high relief with the addition of honeysuckle flowers, hearts, shells, fans, trefoils and the guilloche motif specially designed to suit the new method.

Heavy tumblers were made in both fine quality and tale flint-glass by this method. Tumblers in tale glass, a second quality glass taken from the top and bottom of the melting pot, now toughly annealed, replaced pewter mugs in taverns and other places of public resort. Tumblers at this time were short, broad and heavy-based. In best flint-glass the sharpness and fine detail of the cutting gave to the metal in certain lights a brilliance akin to that of silver. Serving jugs in great variety were moulded for pattern and body shape in open-and-shut de- canter moulds and finished by hand manipulation.

Wax candles, faintly perfumed, burning in cut-glass fixtures were considered

H

the ultimate in Regency illumination. The crystal arms to such fixtures were festooned with ropes of carefully faceted lustres and often the candles rose from flower-calyx sockets. The chandelier of the mansion stateroom now became a vast canopy of pendant lustres closely spaced and entirely enclosing the central shaft, now of metal; from concentric rings fixed to the base sprang several short branches fitted with sockets. These were entirely of glass, except for the rings. Less lavishly there was a central ornamental shaft of glass constructed from blown units, with six, eight, or twelve branches extending from an urn-shaped member near the base. Canopies and base were hung with lustres. Sets of wall lights were entirely of glass, except for the back-plates of gilded brass: there might be as many as a dozen matching lights on the walls of a drawing room in addition to a single magnificent chandelier. These were festooned with strings of lustres. In the 1820's joints in the shaft and the socket holders might also be in gilded brass.

By 1810 candelabra for pier table and mantelshelf had lost their attractive light reflecting finials: instead, every part of the glass surface was diamond-cut, and by 1820 foot, pillar and canopy might be step-cut, the prisms cut at angles best suited for reflecting the light. Lustre drops were now elongated into a drooping slenderness: these were used in association with festoons of smaller lustres. They were succeeded by flat-surfaced hanging prisms more adequately reflecting the greater illumination provided.

The girandole-candlestick was now made with an inverted saucer foot of the same diameter as the canopy, its edges either plain or encircled with short, narrow flutes. Then, in about 1815, came the umbrella canopy, and from a heavy, facet-cut knop rose an expansive saucer-shaped socket with a spreading horizontal rim. The entire surface was diamond-cut in relief. This was followed by the double-cascade girandole-candlestick. In the early 1820's the flat, disc foot was preferred and long lustres resembling thin, pear-shaped icicles each extending almost the length of the body (Pl. 59c).

Desks, dressing-tables and dining-tables during the 1820's might be enriched with glass accessories containing profile portraits, coats-of-arms and other ornaments emitting a silvery brilliance within the glass. These were invented in 1819 by Apsley Pellat and marketed as *crystallo ceramie*. Late Georgians were fascinated by the wide range of glass in which these trifles were embedded: decanters and stoppers, goblets, tumblers, mugs, sugar-basins in tea-caddy sets, ice plates, knife-rests, scent and aromatic vinegar bottles, and wall plaques of celebrities.

Coloured glass in quantity began to enrich the English home from about 1815, its cost being one penny per pound more than clear flint-glass. Bristol blue had been harshly purple in hue because of war-time withdrawal of supplies of Saxon zaffre and smalt, synthetic ultramarine being used as an alternative from about 1805. By about 1820 the use of Saxon smalt was producing a royal-purple tinge. This became known as king's blue when George IV expressed his admiration of a coronation gift of a gilded blue glass spirit set – three labelled decanters, a dozen glasses and a large oval tray of blue glass. It thereupon became a fashionable conceit to make finger-bowls and wine-glass coolers in this metal, the remainder of the table equipage being in fine-quality cut flint-glass. King's blue was costly and found only in blown ware. Pot metal coloured with zaffre was used for cheaper glass. Pale green hock glasses with wide hollow stems were also fashionable, a style revived from the late seventeenth century. They were catalogued as "Hock Glasses, threaded and prunted, 1/- per pound more than wines".

Christmas lights – they were, of course, used for other occasions – were blown in open-and-shut moulds from transparent pot metals of blue, purple, green, ruby red and amber, the surface decorated with a close diamond-quilted pattern. The little oil-burning bowl, without stem or foot, was rimmed to take a wire for hanging.

The colourful trifles in glass associated with the name of Nailsea, but made also at other glass centres such as Tyneside and Stourbridge, gave a touch of luxury to many otherwise austere homes. A pale-green bottle glass blown into flasks and decorated with loops, mottles and flecks in white had been evolved to avoid the high tax payable on flint-glass. By 1815 this low-taxed glass was coloured with metallic oxides to give shades of blue, green, amber and red. These flasks in flattened baluster forms were produced in large numbers: for the most part they were sold as containers of toilet waters. For toilet water too, was the gimmel flask – a twin flask with two containers and spouts. Some were given a crimped or petal foot for standing upright on the toilet table.

Flasks in the form of hand-bellows were made in flint-glass enriched with notches, loops and trailed work and in coloured glass such as blue or red with loops and trailed work in white enamel. Giant bellows flasks, a foot or more in height, for mantelshelf or dressing-table, were made, their nozzles expanded into deep saucer shapes and crimped. These were filled with perfumed water, which pleasantly scented the room.

Coloured glass bells with clappers in clear flint-glass had a delightful resonant tone and were used on the table to summon a servant or in the hall to summon the family at meal-times. These were made in pot-metals, handle and bell in contrasting colours.

Among the larger ornaments intended to hang on parlour walls during the 1820's were slender poignards and dress swords; coaching horns, measuring forty to forty-five inches in length and often containing three loops; giant tobacco pipes; riding-crops. There were walking sticks (Pl. 60A), too, and canes and shepherds' crooks, red, white and blue spirals being particularly popular. These were tapered at the ends and might be enriched with spiral threads in red, blue, green, amber or white opaque glass. Hollow canes of clear flint-glass were filled with comfits and the ferrules plugged with cork.

Rolling-pins in bottle-glass continued their traditional use as salt containers until about 1820, hanging in the kitchen fireplace to keep dry the expensive salt then burdened with a tax of thirty times its cost of manufacture. Some were sold filled with tea or sugar. By 1815, made in clear flint-glass, rolling-pins might be filled with colourful comfits, and became attractive gifts for sweethearts. Soon they were being gilded, painted and engraved with mottoes and good wishes. Such rolling-pins were regarded as lucky charms and were not removed from the wall until pastry was being prepared ceremoniously for a wedding breakfast. They were also advertised as "sailors' charms".

Glass spheres, known as watch-balls, in which a whole room was mirrored in miniature, continued to be made, but with some distortion in the reflections. Nailsea also made balls in coloured glass intended as jug-covers to prevent the entry of insects and dust. From 1820 these might be spotted, looped or spiralled in opaque white.

EARLY VICTORIAN

DURING the eighteen-thirties and early 'forties clear lead crystal with cut decoration continued to be the characteristic product of the British glass factories. This was largely due to the international success of the English and Irish cut crystal of the earlier part of the century; but it can also be attributed in some degree to the heavy excise duty on glass and the restrictive methods used in its collection which tended to limit experiments in new methods of colouring glass and of decorating it.

The early nineteenth-century version of mitre cutting, with its diaper patterns of deeply cut diamonds arranged predominantly in horizontal motifs, became traditional to British cut crystal work and has survived in its essentials to the present day. In the more fashionable work of the 'thirties and early 'forties, however, a distinctive stylistic development was based upon the use of flat or curved surface cutting, implying the removal of slices from the surface of a vessel, rather than upon the criss-cross of mitre grooves. In this phase straight vertical motifs were preferred, and these were achieved most frequently by broadly hollowed or pillared flutes or more simply by flat vertical facets. The use of such motifs affected not merely the decoration of objects but also their shapes. Perhaps because it was easier to cut the broad flutes or facets on surfaces which curved only in one direction, the shapes tended to be ones with angular profiles. The barrel-shaped decanters of the earlier part of the century became basically cylindrical in shape; whilst the neck rings of the older type tended to disappear, probably because they interfered with a sense of simple vertical pattern. These characteristics can already be seen in the pattern drawings of about 1830 which belonged to Samuel Miller, foreman cutter at the Waterford factory,[1] and their development in the 'thirties and 'forties can be noticed in surviving pattern-books in English factories.

The angular broad-fluted work represented in glassware the last phase of the heavy formal Empire style which had affected all the decorative arts of the early nineteenth century. As such it stood in sharp contrast to the revived rococo style which had already developed by the 'twenties in British porcelain and silverwork as a reaction against the Empire formality. Rococo motifs could scarcely be used

[1] M. S. Dudley Westropp, *Irish Glass*, 1920, p. 56, etc.

directly in cut crystal work, but the accompanying feeling for curving shapes and for curved and often asymmetrical motifs was a minor element in British glasswork during the 'thirties and was to become predominant during the later 'forties and 'fifties. Decanters or water-carafes with globular bodies were beginning to appear in the 'thirties alongside the many straight-sided cylindrical examples. The decanter with a globular body and tall slender neck was a natural glass shape which had appeared at many different times in the history of blown glass; and although the Early Victorian version of it was often decorated with facet or mitre cutting, it was best produced in comparatively thin glass with decoration of shallow-cut hollows or else of engraving. It is interesting to notice that of the six clear glass decanters which happen to be illustrated in the *Journal of Design and Manufactures* from the display at the Birmingham Exhibition of 1849, five are globular or squat-globular in shape. One of these, by George Bacchus and Sons of Birmingham, has engraved decoration, another by W. H., B. and J. Richardson of Stourbridge is mainly decorated by a pattern of cut hollows, and the others, by Lloyd and Summerfield of Birmingham and by Bacchus, are decorated by cutting over their whole surface. An analogous curvilinear shape was that of the champagne glass with hemispherical bowl, which was in fashion by the early 'thirties.[1] By the middle of the century wine-glasses of all sorts were being made in a variety of curved, and often ogee-curved, forms.

The removal of the excise duty on glass in 1845 was followed by an enthusiastic development of deep mitre cutting on objects suitable for making in thick glass, and the more ambitious of this work included the use of curvilinear motifs such as that produced by Richardsons for the 1851 Exhibition (Pl. 64A). On the other hand, almost immediately after the 1851 Exhibition cut crystal work began to lose its fashionable standing, and during the remainder of the 'fifties, and beyond, new designs of this nature tended to be somewhat unobtrusive, such for instance as over-all patterns of small widely-spaced stars. The profiles of vessels made in the middle and later 'fifties were predominantly globular or curvilinear; and twisted work was beginning to be common, especially as a means of forming the handles of vessels.

Engraving. Throughout the Early Victorian period decoration by engraving was becoming increasingly popular. In the 'thirties engraving was being carried out in Dudley by the Herbert family, and particularly by William Herbert, for the firm of Thomas Hawkes of Dudley. Around the 'forties the Wood family of engravers were working in Stourbridge, and Thomas Wood was among the independent exhibitors at the 1851 Exhibition. Of more specialized and local interest was the engraved work, mostly representing Sunderland Bridge, which was carried out in Sunderland on local glass in the 'thirties and 'forties by Robert Haddock and Robert Pyle. Probably the most outstanding engraved pieces shown at the

---

[1] W. A. Thorpe, *History of English and Irish Glass*, Vol. I, 1929, p. 314.

1851 Exhibition were the goblets with deep floral motifs designed (and perhaps engraved) by W. J. Muckley for Richardsons (Pl. 62A), and the engraved versions of Greek "oenochoe" jug shapes which were commissioned and shown by the London firm of dealers J. G. Green and were perhaps made by Bacchus of Birmingham. The latter included a rare example of finely engraved figure-work (Pl. 62B). Flower and plant motifs varied from tight bunches in a style borrowed from porcelain painting to loose over-all running patterns which appeared equally in the late 'forties on pottery and silverwork. Probably in reaction against the excessively deep mitre cutting of the years around the middle of the century and against the cheap pressed-glass imitations of cutting, engraving became by far the most fashionable method of decoration during a long period following the 1851 Exhibition. In the 'fifties engraving was used for a wide range of wares from services with simple patterned edgings to elaborate prestige pieces closely decorated with Renaissance arabesques. The great vogue for engraving began to attract craftsmen from Central Europe. Prominent among these was J. H. B. Millar, a Bohemian, who towards the end of the 'fifties established in Edinburgh an important firm of engravers which was staffed initially by fellow Bohemian craftsmen.

Fig. 44. Glassware by George Bacchus & Sons at the Birmingham Exhibition, 1849.
Journal of Design and Manufactures (11, 8).

Fig. 45. Pressed-glass fruit dish
made by George Bacchus
& Sons of Birmingham, 1850.

*Journal of Design and
Manufactures*
(IV, 94).

Engraving by acid etching was used commercially in the 'thirties by Thomas Hawkes of Dudley. It was being used by at least one firm in Stourbridge about the early 'forties, and in the 'fifties further experiments were made by Benjamin Richardson (of the Richardson firm which in the later 'fifties was being operated under his name alone). It was not, however, until the 'sixties that extensive use came to be made of the process in this country.

Colour. The styles of cut and engraved glassware which have been described so far were mostly made in the fine clear lead glass for which the glassmakers of this country had already achieved an international reputation. Contemporary British accounts of the glass in international exhibitions never failed to remark upon the superior quality of the British glass material, and the material was naturally seen to its best advantage when it was used clear and uncoloured. In the Central European glassmaking areas of Bohemia and south-east Germany a reaction against British cut crystal had resulted during the 'twenties and 'thirties in a remarkable development in the use of coloured glasses. The techniques and styles associated with the Central European coloured glass work, of this so-called "Biedermeier" period, were taken up by glass factories in western European countries and particularly by those of France. About the later 'thirties coloured glass was being used in British factories for simple cased, or layered, work and as an alternative material for pieces normally made in uncoloured glass. The firm of Thomas Hawkes were producing semi-opaque white glassware with gilt decoration in the mid-'thirties, and glasses engraved through silver stain were being made in Stourbridge about the early 'forties. But it was not until the removal of the excise in 1845 that the British glassmakers suddenly found themselves free to participate fully in the international coloured-glass styles. The leading spirit in this movement seems to have been Benjamin Richardson, and already in the Manchester Exhibition at the end of 1845 the main interest of the big display by the Richardson firm was in coloured, opal, cased and painted glasses.

Other firms followed rapidly to exploit this field of glasswork. Even the Birmingham firm of F. and C. Osler, mainly known for large-scale work in crystal glass, was found showing opal flower vases with relief painted decoration at the Royal Polytechnic Institution Exhibition of 1848. At the Birmingham Exhibition of 1849 the great majority of the glasses of the Birmingham firms George Bacchus and Sons and Rice Harris and Son, as well as those of Richardsons of Stourbridge, showed the use of colour in one form or another. The fashion reached its culmination at the 1851 Exhibition where almost all the important glass manufacturers in the country were seen to be making plain coloured, cased or opal glassware. In the Exhibition catalogue the longest list of colours is that of Rice Harris, which is given as "opal, alabaster, turquoise, amber, canary, topaz, chrysoprase, pink, blue, light and dark ruby, black, brown, green, purple, etc."

Coloured glasses might be used for work in any of the current styles of uncoloured glasswork. Perhaps the most characteristic use of plain coloured glass was for comparatively small objects, toilet bottles and the like, in the sharply angular shapes with broad vertical facet cutting which were associated with the contemporary Bohemian coloured glass. The most dramatic use of coloured glasses, however, was in the cased glass of the period, which was also used largely in styles derived from the Biedermeier glass of Central Europe. In cased glass a semi-opaque white was frequently used as the outer layer, or else as an intermediate layer to give emphasis to the change of colour betweeen, say, clear blue glass on the outside and uncoloured glass on the inside. Such glasses were always decorated by cutting through the outer layer or layers of glass. The cuttings were usually spaced to leave between them undisturbed areas of the outer layer, and cut hollows and hollow flutes were often contrived in a manner which was suggestive of the lights of a Gothic traceried window and which accorded well with the neo-Gothic taste of the period (Pl. 62A). The richness of effect might be further enhanced by painting or engraving on the glass exposed in the cut-away areas, or by gilding on the undisturbed areas of an outer white layer. Another use of cased glass was to give emphasis to engraving. A thin outer layer of clear coloured glass was used as a field through which a pattern was engraved on to the uncoloured body beneath. For this purpose casing had much the same effect as staining, but the depth of the colour made it more suitable for use with comparatively deep engraving. A notable use of this technique was in some at least of the Richardson engraved work associated with W. J. Muckley, which has already been mentioned (Pl. 62A).

The opalines, or vessels made throughout of semi-opaque glass, appeared mostly in styles which were distinct from those of plain coloured or cased glass. Since this material was both coloured and obscured, there was little to gain by cutting it, and makers tended therefore to use it in natural flowing shapes. A current Central European style of two-colour opalines was represented in the work of Richardsons and probably of other Midland factories. White and green opal glasses were combined in the same vessels, the green being used in shapes suggestive of leaves for overhanging rims and other extruding parts. On the other hand, when the British glassmakers were concerned in producing painted and gilt opal glasses, their attention was attracted by the work of the French factories rather than by those of Central Europe. Large white opal vases with floral painting made by Richardsons around 1851 are scarcely distinguishable in general style from the more ambitious French painted vases of the period (Pl. 63B). Most of the painted opalines were of white opal or of alabaster glass; and some of the most attractive of this work appeared on jugs and vases with low-bellied forms which are reminiscent of contemporary jug shapes in pottery. Richardson examples were often painted with friezes of classical figures or with monochrome scenes; and also printed decoration was often used on opalines of this sort.

The fashion for enamel painting did not necessarily imply the use of semi-opaque glasses. The Richardson firm in particular was responsible for a considerable amount of painting on objects of clear transparent glass; and this was the most favoured medium for the glass designs commissioned by Henry Cole around 1847 for his "Summerly's Art Manufactures". The latter included glasses painted with a much-imitated motif of water-plants, which were designed by the painter Richard Redgrave and made by the firm of J. F. Christy of Lambeth (Pl. 63A).

The belated British participation in the coloured-glass styles of the mid-century was momentous in its time, but it was also short-lived. Two other influences upon British glasswork of the period need to be considered – those of Greek pottery and of Venetian glass. Neither of these influences was dramatic in its immediate effects, but both were to be of lasting significance in the developing tradition of modern British glassware.

Greek forms. The somewhat academic Victorian revival of Greek pottery forms was reflected in many of the details of glass shapes and decorations after the removal of the excise duty in 1845. The Greek pinched mouth, for instance, became a common feature of the opal and alabaster glass jugs. About 1847 a London dealer, a Mr Giller of Holborn, was producing (through Thomas Webb of Stourbridge and the London decorating firm of Thomas Battam) painted glassware which was deliberately shaped and decorated in the manner of Greek pottery. Other painted glass versions of Greek pottery were shown at the 1851 Exhibition by Davis, Greathead and Green of Stourbridge. The use of Greek jug shapes in clear glass with engraved decoration has already been mentioned in the instance of the display of the dealers J. G. Green at the 1851 Exhibition (Pl. 62B), and it was from sources such as this that the high-shouldered decanters and claret jugs of the later part of the century were derived.

Venetian influence. The Venetian influence is less easily defined. The word "Venetian" occurs in the 1851 Exhibition catalogue in descriptions of the work of the Richardson firm, of Davis, Greathead and Green, of Rice Harris, and of Apsley Pellat; but it is difficult to find any common denominator among this work other than a certain freedom or eccentricity of style. Glasses made by Apsley Pellat were described as Venetian in the 1847 *Art-Union* with apparently little reason other than that they were engraved with Renaissance arabesque patterns; whilst the Venetian element in the same firm's "Anglo-Venetian" glasses at the 1851 Exhibition consisted in their being frosted and gilt. An important feature in the work of the Bacchus firm about the middle of the century was the use of multi-coloured threading in the stems of wine-glasses, and these were often also convoluted (Pl. 64B). At the 1851 Exhibition threaded glass was also shown by Rice Harris, and elaborately convoluted stems were a feature of wine-glasses shown by Lloyd and Summerfield. The style of Venetian glass in the sense of a style using rapidly formed plastic shapes, was strongly advocated by Ruskin in the second volume of his *Stones of Venice* (1853); and this concept was applied by the architect Philip Webb when, around 1860, he was designing table-glasses to be made for William Morris by James Powell and Sons of London.

Novelties. A feature of early Victorian glasswork was the appearance of various sorts of glass novelties, which in effect meant the use of glass for unexpected purposes or the use of unusual glass techniques for the sake of their interest as curiosities. Apsley Pellat's "cameo incrustations", or small white paste images enclosed within clear glass, were, in this country, a novelty of the early 'twenties, although the knowledge of them survived sufficiently for them to be included in the firm's display at the 1851 Exhibition. Around the middle of the century glass busts were being made by two of the Birmingham firms, F. and C. Osler and Lloyd and Summerfield. These were produced in moulds; and those by Osler, at least, were given a frosted surface by abrading. A novelty of the same period were the double-walled vessels with silvering on the interior surfaces, which gave an opportunity for interesting effects of reflection and colour. The patent for this method of manufacture was taken out in 1849 by F. Hale Thomson and Edward Varnish, and the vessels were apparently made at the factory of James Powell and Sons.

The most striking of the Early Victorian novelties, however, were the glass paper-weights enclosing ingenious coloured patterns. The vogue for paper-weights came to this country from France, where they had been made in great numbers since 1845. A writer in the first volume of the *Journal of Design and Manufactures* in 1849 gives a clear indication of the extent of the popular fancy for paper-weights and of the firm which was responsible for developing their manufacture in this country: "It were to be wished that Messrs Bacchus had been a little earlier in the manufacture of their Glass Paper Weights, for the specimens we have recently seen at their works are quite equal in transparency, colour, skilful arrangements of parts, and ingenuity of make, to the foreign works with which stationers' and fancy shops have been and are so crowded." Most of the paper-weights which can be presumed to have been made in this country during the mid-century years are of the "millefiori" variety, whereby an internal pattern was built up by arranging small coloured glass canes in concentric circles; and once acquired, the millefiori technique was used in the same manner for other objects, such as standing inkwells and door-knobs, which offered similar opportunities for the use of thick glass as a means of magnifying the internal pattern.

Pressed glass. Most of the fine glasswork of the period was made, as it is today, by the traditional methods of hand-craftsmanship; although some, such as opaline glasses with relief decoration, would be produced by blowing into moulds. This was a period in which the methods of moulding were greatly extended for the making of cheap glassware, and in particular it was the period in which the process of press-moulding was first developed for the production of dishes and other open shapes. The method of pressing glass between a mould and a plunger appears to have been mainly an American invention. In this country it was being extensively used from the early 'thirties onwards by a number of Midland firms, notably Thomas Hawkes, Bacchus (known during most of the 'thirties as Bacchus and Green), and Rice Harris; it was also presumably used by Apsley Pellat, who patented a small modification to the process in 1831. In America the pressed glass of the 'thirties and 'forties was mostly decorated in the "lacy" style with elaborate relief patterns on finely stippled grounds, and a somewhat similar free style of relief decoration was used on pressed glass in France. Some of the early British patterns for pressed glass were no doubt of this sort; but it seems probable that the majority were in imitation of cut crystal styles, and this was perhaps natural in the country to which cut crystal was native (Fig. 45). Identifiable pieces of British pressed glass in "lacy" and similar styles are usually found to belong to a later phase about the 'seventies and 'eighties when much of the British pressed-glass industry was concentrated in the north-east of England.

For Further Reading

POTTERY AND PORCELAIN

Catalogue of the Glaisher Collection (2 vols), by Bernard Rackham, C.U.P., Cambridge, 1934, New York, 1935.

Concise Encyclopedia of English Pottery and Porcelain, by Wolf Mankowitz and Reginald G. Haggar, Deutsch, London, and Hawthorn, New York, 1957.

Early Staffordshire Pottery, by Bernard Rackham, Faber, London, 1951; Pitman, New York, 1952.

English Delftware, by F. H. Garner, Faber, London, and Pitman, New York, 1948.

English Porcelain of the Eighteenth Century, by J. L. Dixon, Faber, London, and Pitman, New York, 1952.

English Pottery and Porcelain, by W. B. Honey, Black, London, 1947.

GLASS

English Glass, by W. B. Honey, Collins, London, 1946.

English Glass, by W. A. Thorpe, Black, London, 1949; Macmillan, New York, 1961.

A History of English and Irish Glass (2 vols), by W. A. Thorpe, Medici Society, London, 1929.

History of Old English Glass, by Francis Buckley, Benn, London, 1925.

Index

PLATE IA. Cistern of green lead-glazed earthenware, with Royal Arms of England as borne by Henry VII, and initials of Henry VII and Elizabeth of York. English, about 1525–30. Ht 12¾ in. *Victoria and Albert Museum.*

PLATE IB. Mug, green lead-glazed earthenware. English, third quarter of sixteenth century. Ht 4⁷⁄₁₀ in. *British Museum.*

PLATE IC. Dish of green lead-glazed earthenware, with Royal Arms of England, from the site of Eltham Palace. English, about 1540. *H.M. Office of Works.*

PLATES: 2A. Tankard, brown lead-glazed earthenware, in embossed and engraved silver-gilt mount. London hall-mark for 1547–8. About 1545. Ht 7⅝ in. *Victoria and Albert Museum.* 2B. Tankard, tinglazed earthenware ("Malling jug") in silver-gilt mounts with the London hall-mark for 1549–50. About 1545–50. Ht 6⅕ in. *British Museum.*

PLATE 2C. Dish, tin-glazed earthenware. Made in London, dated 1600. Diameter 10⅛ in. *London Museum.*

B

C

PLATES: 3A. Tankard, dark-brown lead-glazed earthenware ("Cistercian" ware). Found at Youlgreave and probably made in Derbyshire, sixteenth century. Ht 11½ in. *Fitzwilliam Museum, Cambridge.* 3B. Candlestick, green lead-glazed earthenware, with the Pegasus badge of the Inner Temple impressed. Late sixteenth century. Ht 5⅜ in. *Victoria and Albert Museum.* 3C. Two-handled cup, dark-brown lead-glazed earthenware with white " slip" decoration. Probably Yorkshire; mid-sixteenth century. Ht 6⅜ in. *Yorkshire Museum, York.* 3D. "Tyg", dark-brown lead-glazed earthenware ("Cistercian" ware). Dated 1599. Ht. 5⅜ in. *British Museum.* 3E. "Tyg", dark-brown lead-glazed earthenware ("Cistercian" ware) with white "slip" decoration. Sixteenth century. Ht 3 in. *Victoria and Albert Museum.* 3F. "Tyg", dark-brown lead-glazed earthenware ("Cistercian" ware). Found and probably made at Tickenhall, Derbyshire; sixteenth century. Ht 4⅜ in.
Victoria and Albert Museum.

E

F

PLATE 4A. A bowl of blue-and-white porcelain, mounted in silver-gilt by a gold-smith working about 1583–90. Originally in the possession of Lord Treasurer Cecil. Chinese, period of Wan Li (1573–1610). *Courtesy of the Metropolitan Museum, New York.*

PLATE 4B. Bowl, celadon porcelain with incised decoration, set in an English silver-gilt mount. Chinese, period of the Ming dynasty (1368–1643). Ht 4¾ in. *Courtesy of the Warden and Fellows of New College, Oxford.*

PLATE 7A. Tankard, lead-glazed earthenware with slip decoration. Probably made in London, mid-seventeenth century. Ht 7¼ in. *London Museum.*

PLATE 7B. Mug, lead-glazed earthenware with trailed and combed slip decoration. Staffordshire, dated 1701. Ht 4¼ in. *Victoria and Albert Museum.*

PLATE 8A. Dish, lead-glazed earthenware with slip decoration. By Thomas Toft, of Staffordshire, about 1675. Diameter 17¼ in. *Victoria and Albert Museum.*

PLATE 8B. Model of a cradle, lead-glazed earthenware with trailed slip decoration. Staffordshire, dated 1700. Length 16 in. *Fitzwilliam Museum, Cambridge.*

PLATE 8C. Posset-pot, greenish-brown lead-glazed earthenware. Inscribed "William and mary Goldsmith". S. Wilts, dated 1697. Ht 8¾ in. *Fitzwilliam Museum, Cambridge.*

PLATE 9A. Dish, lead-glazed earthenware with trailed slip decoration. Staffordshire, late seventeenth or early eighteenth century. Diameter 13 in. *Northampton Museum.*

PLATE 9B. Bowl, polychrome delftware. Perhaps Bristol, early eighteenth century. Diameter 12 in. *Victoria and Albert Museum.*

PLATE 9C. Posset-pot, delftware painted in blue. Lambeth, dated 1685. Ht $13\frac{1}{2}$ in. *Fitzwilliam Museum, Cambridge.*

PLATE 10A. Charger, polychrome delftware.
London, dated 1635. Diameter 19 in. *Victoria
and Albert Museum.*

PLATE 10B. Wine-bottle ("Bellarmine"), salt-glazed stoneware
with applied moulded relief decoration, about 1680. Found on the
site of John Dwight's factory at
Fulham. Ht 8 in.
Victoria and Albert Museum.

PLATE 10C. Charger, polychrome delftware.
Lambeth, about 1680. Diameter 13¾ in.
Victoria and Albert Museum.

PLATE 11B. Teapot, brown salt-glazed stoneware with enamelled decoration. Staffordshire, about 1700. Ht 5½ in. *Victoria and Albert Museum.*

PLATE 11A. Figure of Lydia Dwight, salt-glazed stoneware. By John Dwight, Fulham, about 1673–4. Ht 11¼ in. *Victoria and Albert Museum.*

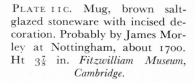

PLATE 11C. Mug, brown salt-glazed stoneware with incised decoration. Probably by James Morley at Nottingham, about 1700. Ht 3⅞ in. *Fitzwilliam Museum, Cambridge.*

PLATE 12A. Covered jar, porcelain painted in underglaze blue. Chinese, second quarter of the seventeenth century. Ht approx. 13 in. *Hampton Court, by gracious permission of Her Majesty the Queen.*

PLATE 12B. Covered jar, porcelain painted in polychrome enamels in the "Kakiemon" style. Japanese (Arita), late seventeenth century. Ht 12½ in. *Hampton Court, by gracious permission of Her Majesty the Queen.*

PLATES: 12C. Tankard, porcelain painted in underglaze blue, mounted in a contemporary English silver mount. Chinese, second quarter of seventeenth century. Ht 7½ in. *Victoria and Albert Museum.* 12D. Mug, porcelain with enamelled decoration. Chinese (Tê-hua), late seventeenth century. Ht 3¾ in *Victoria and Albert Museum.*

PLATE 13A. Mug, delftware, painted in blue and inscribed: "IOHN POTTEN & SVSANNA 1633". Southwark. Ht 5⅜ in. *Fitzwilliam Museum, Cambridge.*

PLATE 13B. Wine-bottle, delftware, inscribed in blue. London, dated 1647. Ht 4¾ in. *Victoria and Albert Museum.*

PLATE 13C. Teapot, unglazed red stoneware with moulded decoration. Chinese (Yi-hsing); late seventeenth or early eighteenth century. Ht 4⅛ in. *Victoria and Albert Museum.*

PLATES (*right*) : 15A. Plate, delftware, painted in blue on a sprayed manganese-purple ground. Wincanton, 1738. Diameter 8¾ in. *Fitzwilliam Museum, Cambridge.* 15B. Plate, delftware, painted in "Fazackerly" colours within a *bianco-sopra-bianco* border. Probably Bristol, about 1750–60. Diameter 10⅛ in. *Victoria and Albert Museum.*

PLATE 14A. Tray, delftware, painted in blue. Probably Bristol, 1743. Diameter 14 in. *Victoria and Albert Museum.*

PLATE 14B. Bowl delftware, painted in colours. Lambeth, about 1760. Diameter 12 in. *Collection of R. J. Charleston.*

A

B

PLATE 15C. Puzzle-jug, delftware, painted in blue. Bristol, about 1760. *Bristol Art Gallery.*

PLATE 15D. Food-warmer, delftware, painted in blue. Probably Bristol, first half of eighteenth century. Ht of stand 5 in. *Victoria and Albert Museum.*

PLATE 16A. Teapot, "agate-ware". Staffordshire, about
1740. Ht 4 in. *Victoria and Albert Museum.*

PLATE 16B. Jug, lead-glazed earthenware,
with the decoration incised through the dark
to the light clay. Staffordshire, 1726. Ht 5⅞
in. *Fitzwilliam Museum, Cambridge.*

PLATE 16C. Figure of lead-glazed earthenware, the glaze dappled with colours. Staffordshire, about 1740. Ht 7$\frac{9}{16}$ in. *Victoria and Albert
Museum.*

PLATE 17A. Teapot, unglazed red
earthenware. Staffordshire, about
1750–60. Ht 5 in. *Victoria and Albert
Museum.*

PLATE 17B. Teapot, dark lead-glazed earthenware with white
relief-decoration. Staffordshire, about 1740. Ht 6 in. *Victoria and
Albert Museum.*

PLATE 18A. Plate, delftware, painted in colours.
Lambeth, 1737. Diameter 8½ in. *Victoria and Albert
Museum.*

PLATE 18B. Teapot, coffee-pot and jug of "Astbury-Whieldon" type and "Jackfield" jug.
Mainly Staffordshire, about 1740–50. *Victoria and Albert Museum.*

PLATE 19A. Plate, lead-glazed earthenware with moulded rim and patches of colour in the glaze. "Whieldon-type"; about 1760. Diameter 9¼ in. *Victoria and Albert Museum.*

PLATE 19B. Two teapots and jug, salt-glazed stoneware. Staffordshire, about 1740–50. *Victoria and Albert Museum.*

PLATE 20A. Mug, brown and buff salt-glazed stoneware with relief decoration. Fulham, 1739. Ht 8½ in.
Victoria and Albert Museum.

PLATE 20B. Loving-cup, brown salt-glazed stoneware.
Nottingham, 1740. Ht 6¾ in. *Victoria and Albert Museum.*

PLATES: 21A. Coffee-pot, salt-glazed stoneware, painted in enamel colours. Staffordshire, about 1760–5. Ht 9½ in. 21B. Mug, salt-glazed stoneware with incised decoration filled in with cobalt-blue ("scratch-blue"). Staffordshire, dated 1758. Ht 5⅝ in. 21C. Teapot in the form of a camel, salt-glazed stoneware. Staffordshire, about 1745. Ht 4½ in. 21D. Mug representing the capture of Portobello by Admiral Vernon in 1739, salt-glazed stoneware with applied moulded relief. Staffordshire, about 1740. Ht 7 in. *Victoria and Albert Museum.*

PLATES: 22A. Group of a Chinaman and Boy, porcelain. Derby, about 1755. Ht 9¼ in.   22B. Figure of a carpenter, porcelain, painted in colours. Chelsea, about 1755. Ht 7¾ in. 22C. Figure symbolic of Spring, porcelain, painted in colours. Chelsea, about 1755. Ht 5¼ in. 22D. Figure of Neptune, porcelain. Bow, about 1755. Ht 6¼ in. *Victoria and Albert Museum.*

PLATES: 23A. Jug, porcelain, painted in colours. Longton Hall, about 1755. Ht 8¾ in. 23B. Tureen in the form of a rabbit, porcelain, painted in colours. Chelsea, about 1755. Length 14¼ in. 23C. Tureen, porcelain. Bow, about 1750–5. Ht 7½ in. 23D. Coffee-pot, porcelain with black transfer-print, "L'Amour", by R. Hancock. Worcester, about 1765. Ht 8¾ in.
Victoria and Albert Museum.

PLATES: 24A. Vase, porcelain, painted in colours. Bow, about 1755. Ht 7⅞ in. 24B. Dish, porcelain, painted in colours in the "Kakiemon" manner. Bow, about 1755. Diameter 9½ in. 24C. Dish, porcelain, painted in colours in the Meissen manner. Chelsea, about 1755. Diameter 16¼ in. 24D. Model of a dovecot, probably a pot-pourri, porcelain, painted in colours. Chelsea, about 1755. Ht 14½ in.
Victoria and Albert Museum.

PLATE 25A. A pair of figures of Turks, after models in Meissen porcelain by Johann Joachim Kaendler. Salt-glazed stoneware, painted with enamel colours, *c.* 1760. *Victoria and Albert Museum.*

PLATE 25B. Coffee-pot, earthenware with mottled glaze ("tortoiseshell" ware). Staffordshire, *c.* 1760. Ht 8½ in. *Victoria and Albert Museum.*

PLATE 26A. Delftware tiles of the eighteenth century, *c.* 1765, in polychrome with *bianco-soprabianco* border. *Bristol Art Gallery.*

PLATE 26B. Jug, modelled by John Voyez, inscribed on the reverse side "Fair Hebe", and signed and dated J. Voyez, 1788. *Victoria and Albert Museum.*

PLATE 26C. "Prince Hal" Toby jug by Ralph Wood, Burslem, *c.* 1765. Height 14 in. *Lord Mackintosh of Halifax Collection.*

PLATE 27A. A plate from the Empress Catherine of Russia Service, cream-ware painted in blackish purple monochrome, the crest in green. Wedgwood, 1773–4. *Hanley Museum, Staffs.*

PLATE 27B. A plate with lilac pink border and gold edging. Painted in the centre with a spray of poppies by William "Quaker" Pegg. These poppies are similar to a spray in Pegg's own sketch book, which has survived and is now in the Derby Museum. Mark, a crown with crossed batons and D. in blue. Derby, *c.* 1800. *G. W. Capell Collection.*

PLATE 28A. Figure of Voltaire in black basaltes ware. Wedgwood, Etruria, *c.* 1777–80. *Victoria and Albert Museum.*

PLATE 28B. Chatelaine, comb and bracelet, coloured jasper ware mounted in cut-steel. Wedgwood, Etruria, *c.* 1786–90. *Josiah Wedgwood and Sons Ltd.*

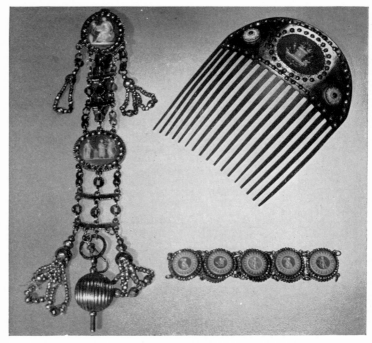

PLATE 29. "The Music Lesson", adapted from a painting by François Boucher, entitled "L'Agréable Leçon", porcelain painted in colours. Mark, an anchor in gold and "R" impressed. Chelsea, *c.* 1765. *Victoria and Albert Museum.*

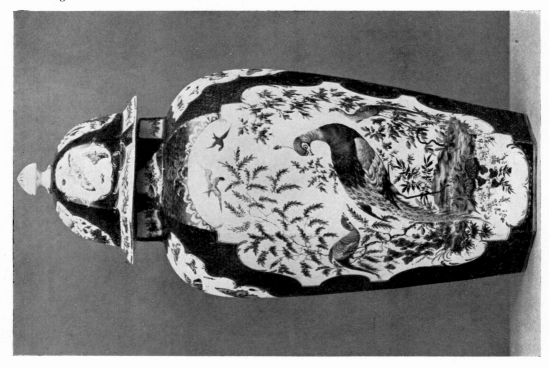

PLATE 30A. A mug, transfer printed in black with a full length of

PLATE 31B. Grouped pieces, representing part of the Royal Family, after a painting by Zoffany, unglazed porcelain (biscuit), Derby, c. 1771. By gracious permission of Her Majesty The Queen.

PLATE 31A. "Chelsea Toys". Chelsea porcelain, c. 1755–65. Victoria and Albert Museum.

PLATE 32A. Pair of Chelsea figures, "The Harvesters". Height 10 in., mark, an anchor in gold, 1758–60. *Collection of Mrs H. Synge-Hutchinson.*

PLATE 32B. The epergne from the service given by King George III and Queen Charlotte to the Duke of Mecklenburg-Strelitz. "Mazarine"-blue ground covered with insects in gold, enclosing panels painted with festoons of flowers. Mark, anchor in gold, Chelsea, *c.* 1763. *By gracious permission of Her Majesty Queen Elizabeth the Queen Mother.*

PLATE 33A. Stone china dish with the well-known "Peacock & Peony" pattern: transfer printed outline over-painted with enamels. Marked SPODE STONE CHINA printed in black. *c.* 1815. *Spode-Copeland Museum, Stoke-on-Trent.*

PLATE 33B. Dessert plate of felspar porcelain bearing the arms of the Goldsmiths' Company in colours and gold within a rim of apple green, its gadroon edge etched with gold. *c.* 1820. *Spode-Copeland Museum, Stoke-on-Trent.*

PLATE 34A. Part of a 33-piece Derby (Bloor) dessert service in bone china, painted in colours with named views.

PLATE 34B. Part of a teaset in bone china with English scenes hand-painted in colours. Wedgwood, 1815. *Wedgwood Museum, Stoke-on-Trent.*

PLATE 35A. Sunderland pottery ewer and basin in mottled pink lustre with transfers of the Wearmouth Bridge and the sailing ship "Northumberland". Marked DIXON & CO. 1813–19. *Lent by Dr J. Dixon Johnson to the Sunderland Museum.*

PLATE 35B. Blue and white transfer-printed earthenware: "The Bridge of Lucano" set in a border of corn, vine and olive motifs. Spode. *c.* 1820. *Spode-Copeland Museum, Stoke-on-Trent.*

PLATE 35C. Swansea porcelain tea warmer heated by spirit lamp or scented mortar candle. 1814–17. *Victoria and Albert Museum.*

PLATE 36A. Ice cream pail with cover and lining. The body and cover are painted with flower groups in natural colours and the crimson ground is ornamented with arabesque embossments in gold. Marked SPODE *967* in red. *c.* 1825. *Spode-Copeland Museum, Stoke-on-Trent.*

PLATE 36B. Bone china plate painted with a country scene. The buff-coloured rim is ornamented with gold spots and brown bell-shaped drops. Marked SPODE impressed. From 1819. *Spode-Copeland Museum, Stoke-on-Trent.*

PLATE 37A. Earthenware jug painted with "The Prince of Wales" stage coach which operated between London and Swansea. Inscribed "Jacob Goodwin 1810". Rim and base decorations are in silver lustre. *Brighton Art Gallery and Museum.*

PLATE 37B. Bone china teapot decorated in the Imari style in deep blues, bold patches of brick red, and green enamels, with gilding. Marked SPODE *967. c.* 1820. *Spode-Copeland Museum, Stoke-on-Trent.*

PLATE 37C. Loving cup in cream coloured earthenware, inscribed "George Barlow, Ecclesfield, 1822". *Courtesy of Clifford Chubb, Esq.*

PLATE 38B. Pearlware figures: Mars in the centre 10¼ in. high, flanked by symbolic figures of Spring and Autumn and two figures of musicians. All marked LEEDS POTTERY. Before 1820. *Leeds City Art Gallery*.

PLATE 38A. Rockingham toby jug in bone china; early 1820's. Formerly in the Penrose collection. *Trust Houses Ltd.*

PLATE 38C. Rockingham china figure ornaments in the form of a dog with puppies and a cat with kittens in baskets. Early 1820's. *Wernher Collection, Luton Hoo.*

PLATE 38D. Staffordshire earthenware figures: a baker's errand boy and a pair of deer with trees, all in painted enamels. *c.* 1825. *Wernher Collection, Luton Hoo.*

PLATE 39A. Blue-printed dish with a fanciful view of Venice, made by Copelands, *c.* 1840. Length 18⅞ in. *Victoria and Albert Museum.*

PLATE 39B. Two examples of white stoneware made by the firm of Charles Meigh, Hanley. The jug is dated 1842; the mug was the subject of a Society of Arts award in 1847. Ht 6¼ in. and 7¼ in. *Victoria and Albert Museum.*

Plate 40B. Staffordshire flat-back figure of Dick Turpin, c. 1850. Ht 11½ in. *Victoria and Albert Museum.*

Plate 40A. Parian porcelain vase with applied flower-work on a drab coloured ground, made by Mintons, c. 1854. Ht 13⅝ in. *Victoria and Albert Museum.*

PLATE 41B. Two of Copelands' parian porcelain statuettes. *Left*, "Innocence" dated 1847 after an original by J. H. Foley; *right*, "Musidora" dated 1857 after William Theed junior. Ht 16⅞ in. and 16¼ in. *Victoria and Albert Museum and W. T. Copeland and Sons.*

PLATE 41A. Coalport vase of porcelain, painted and with applied flower-work; *c.* 1830. Ht 11 in. *Victoria and Albert Museum.*

PLATE 42A. "Limoges ware", made by Kerr and Binns (from 1862 the Worcester Royal Porcelain Company) with white enamel painting by Thomas Bott. Cup and saucer dated 1859; plate dated 1867, with a pattern originally used on this ware in the middle 'fifties. Diameter of plate 10⅜ in. *Victoria and Albert Museum and Worcester Royal Porcelain Company.*

PLATE 42B. Porcelain standing dish with parian figures representing "Bottom and the Tinker", from the Shakespeare service shown by Kerr and Binns, Worcester, at the Dublin Exhibition, 1853. Ht 15¾ in. *Worcester Royal Porcelain Company.*

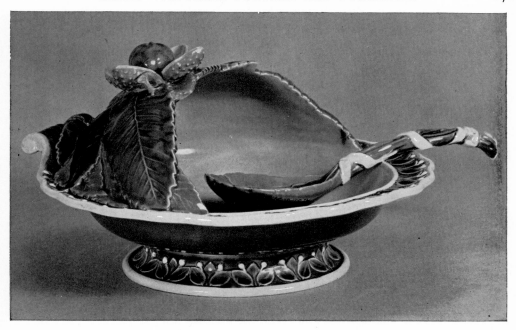

PLATE 43A. "Majolica" chestnut dish with spoon, made by Mintons, *c.* 1855. Diam. 9⅞ in. *Victoria and Albert Museum.*

PLATE 43B. Part of an earthenware tea service designed by Henry Cole and made by Mintons. The service gained a Society of Arts award in 1846. Ht of teapot 6 in. *Victoria and Albert Museum.*

A   B   C

PLATES: 44A. Wine-glass with gilt decoration including two coats-of-arms (one that of the Vintners' Company) and the name Wenyfrid Geares. English, dated 1590. Ht 7½ in. *The Duke of Northumberland*. 44B. Goblet, enamelled glass set in silver-gilt foot bearing the London hall-mark for 1547–8. Venetian, early sixteenth century. Ht 9 in. *The Founders' Company and the Goldsmiths' Company*. 44C. Wine-glass, engraved with the diamond-point, perhaps by Anthony de Lysle. Decorated with the Royal Arms as borne by Queen Elizabeth I, and the names JOHN JONE *Dier*. English, dated 1581. Ht 8⅛ in. *Victoria and Albert Museum*.

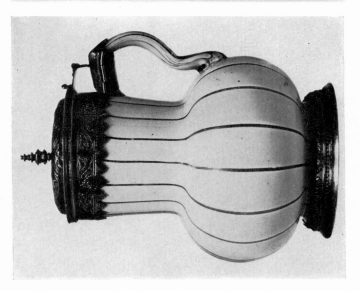

A   B   C

PLATES: 45A. Mug of glass with *latticinio* stripes, the silver-gilt mounts bearing the London hall-mark for 1548. Venetian, *c.* 1540. Ht 5¼ in. *British Museum.* 45B. Bottle of hexagonal section, in green glass. Found and made in Woodchester, Glos., about 1600. Ht 5½ in. *City Museum, Gloucester.* 45C. Flask of green glass with "wrythen" ribbed decoration. Said to have been excavated in Oxford. Perhaps English, *c.* 1600. Ht 4⅜ in. *Victoria and Albert Museum.*

PLATE 46A. "A Financial Transaction", detail from an oil-painting by Lucas Cranach, the Elder (1472–1553), showing a colourless glass beaker of about 1530, probably made in the Netherlands. *Nationalmuseum, Stockholm.*

PLATE 46B. "Family Group", oil-painting probably by Maarten van Heemskerck (1498–1574), showing a wine-glass probably made in Venice or perhaps in the Netherlands during the second quarter of the sixteenth century. *Staatliche Kunstsammlungen, Kassel.*

PLATE 47A. Posset-pot, glass. English, about 1685. Ht 12¼ in. *Courtesy of Donald H. Beves, Esq.*

PLATE 47B. Jug, glass. Probably made at the Savoy glass-house of George Ravenscroft, about 1680. Ht 10⅞ in. *Victoria and Albert Museum.*

PLATE 48A. Roemer, glass, with applied impressed "prunts". London, about 1680–5. Ht 7⅞ in. *Victoria and Albert Museum.*

PLATE 48B. Detail from portrait of Erasmus by Holbein, showing (top right) a glass bottle, perhaps Venetian, the adjacent book gives the date 1523. *The Earl of Radnor.*

PLATE 48C. Goblet, glass, the hollow stem enclosing a sixpence of King William III, dated 1690. English, last decade of the seventeenth century. Ht 9 in. *Victoria and Albert Museum.*

PLATE 49A. Wine-glass, English
or Venetian for the English market,
middle of the seventeenth century.
Ht 6 in. *Victoria and Albert Museum.*

PLATE 49B. Wine-glass, English,
early eighteenth century. Ht 7⅛ in.
Victoria and Albert Museum.

PLATE 49C. "Flute-glass", engraved
with the diamond-point. Arms of
England and Scudamore. English,
c. 1650. Ht 13½ in. *London Museum.*

PLATE 50A. Oil-painting by William Dobson, said to show Prince Rupert and Col. Murray persuading Col. Russell to rejoin the Royalists. In the wine-glass a red wine. *Courtesy of Lord Sandys*.

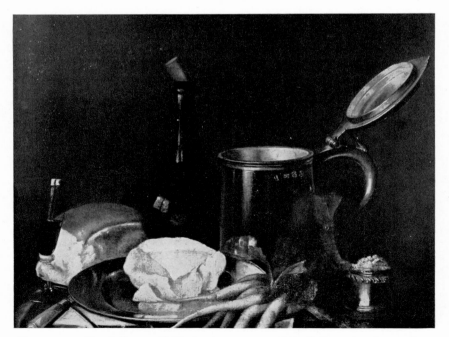

PLATE 50B. Detail from still-life in the manner of E. Collier, showing a silver tankard bearing the English hall-mark for 1688, a wine-glass, and a black glass bottle. English, late seventeenth century. *Victoria and Albert Museum*.

PLATES: 51A. Sweetmeat glass with cut decoration. About 1730–40. Ht 6 in.
51B. Bowl engraved with arms of the Ferguson-Davie family, about 1760.
Diameter 8½ in. *Victoria and Albert Museum.*

PLATES: 51C. Wine-glass, about 1725. Ht 6⅞ in. 51D. Candlestick, glass with
shouldered stem. About 1740. Ht 10½ in. *Victoria and Albert Museum.*

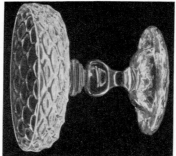

PLATE 52D.   Sweetmeat glass, second quarter of eighteenth century. Ht 4⅝in.

Victoria and Albert Museum.

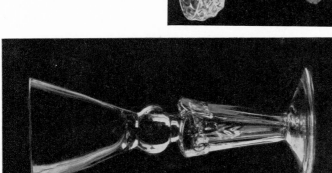

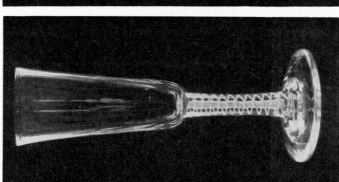

PLATES: 52B. Ale-glass with opaque-white twist stem. About 1760. Ht 9 in. 52C. Wine-glass, the pedestal stem moulded with the words GOD SAVE KING G. About 1715. Ht 6⅛ in.

PLATE 52A. Toastmaster's glass with deceptive bowl. Early eighteenth century. Ht 6⅛ in.

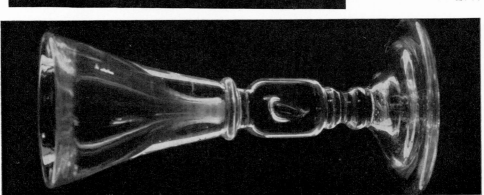

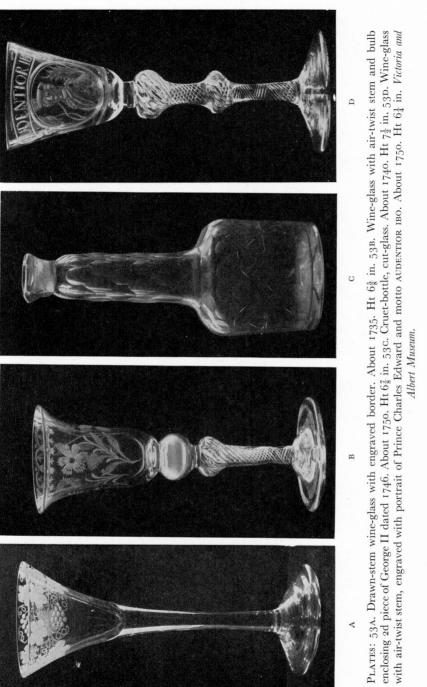

PLATES: 53A. Drawn-stem wine-glass with engraved border. About 1735. Ht 6⅝ in. 53B. Wine-glass with air-twist stem and bulb enclosing 2d piece of George II dated 1746. About 1750. Ht 6⅞ in. 53C. Cruet-bottle, cut-glass. About 1740. Ht 7½ in. 53D. Wine-glass with air-twist stem, engraved with portrait of Prince Charles Edward and motto AUDENTIOR IBO. About 1750. Ht 6¼ in. *Victoria and Albert Museum.*

PLATES: 54A. Decanter. About 1730–40. Ht 9 in. *Victoria and Albert Museum.*
54B. Jar of opaque-white glass painted in enamels, perhaps in Staffordshire.
About 1760. *Ashmolean Museum, Oxford.*

PLATE 54C. Portrait of the Duke of Newcastle and the Earl of Lincoln by
Sir Godfrey Kneller, *c.* 1718. *National Portrait Gallery.*

PLATE 55. Trade-card of Maydwell and Windle, glass-sellers in the Strand, *c.* 1770.

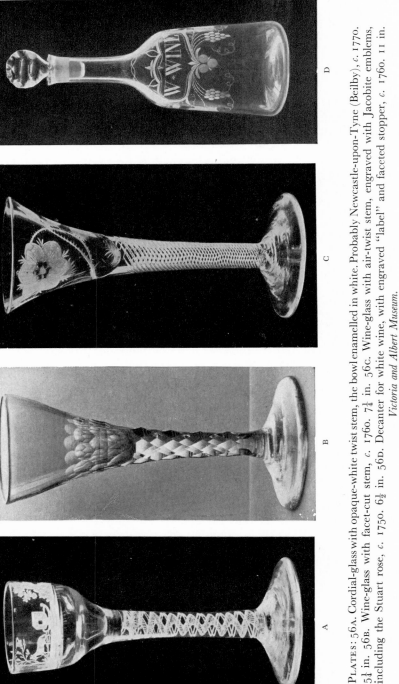

PLATES: 56A. Cordial-glass with opaque-white twist stem, the bowl enamelled in white. Probably Newcastle-upon-Tyne (Beilby), *c.* 1770. 5¼ in. 56B. Wine-glass with facet-cut stem, *c.* 1760. 7¼ in. 56C. Wine-glass with air-twist stem, engraved with Jacobite emblems, including the Stuart rose, *c.* 1750. 6½ in. 56D. Decanter for white wine, with engraved "label" and faceted stopper, *c.* 1760. 11 in. *Victoria and Albert Museum.*

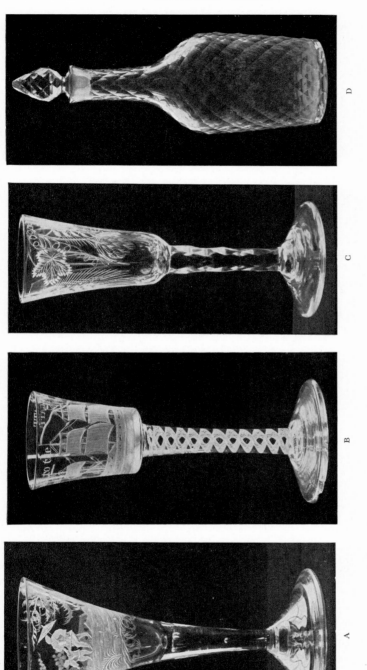

PLATES: 57A. Wine-glass engraved with *chinoiserie* subject, *c.* 1760. 9⅜ in. 57B. Wine-glass with opaque-white twist stem. Engraved with representation of a frigate and inscription: "Success to the Eagle Frigate. John Knill, Commander", *c.* 1760. 6½ in. 57C. Ale-glass with faceted stem, the bowl engraved with hops and barley, *c.* 1760. 7½ in. 57D. Decanter and stopper, cut in facets, *c.* 1760. 12 in. *Victoria and Albert Museum.*

PLATE 58. Cut-glass chandelier from Wroxton Abbey, Oxfordshire, *c.* 1810.
6 ft. *Victoria and Albert Museum.*

PLATE 59A. *Crystallo ceramie* cup with portraits of George III and the Prince Regent between panels of fine diamond-cutting: made by Apsley Pellat. Early 1820's. *By gracious permission of Her Majesty the Queen.*

PLATE 59B. Rummer for serving toddy engraved with scenes in the life of a butcher. This view shows him on his way to deliver meat to a country house. 1810. *Courtesy of O. N. Norris, Esq.*

PLATE 59C. Pair of girandole candlesticks in flint-glass with revolving canopies, gilded metal stem units, and round feet radially cut beneath. Late 1820's.
Corning Museum of Glass, Corning, N.Y.

PLATE 60B. Heavy flint-glass hollow-ware lavishly cut, the forms of cutting being variously combined. 1820's.

PLATE 60A. Glass walking sticks: the majority are solid with coloured 'twist' decoration, others are hollow and filled with "hundreds and thousands" in bands of alternating colours. 1810–30. *Courtesy the Rt. Hon. Alan Lennox-Boyd.*

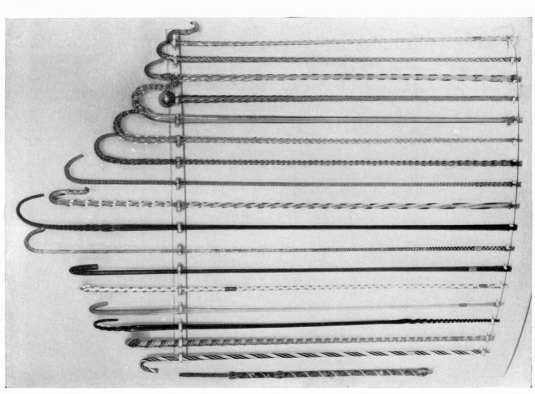

PLATE 61A. Jug, honey-pot and toilet table bottle decorated with large relief diamonds and prismatic cutting.

PLATE 61B. Ormolu and glass chandelier. In the drawing room at Gadebridge Park, Hemel Hempstead, Hertfordshire. *c.* 1810.

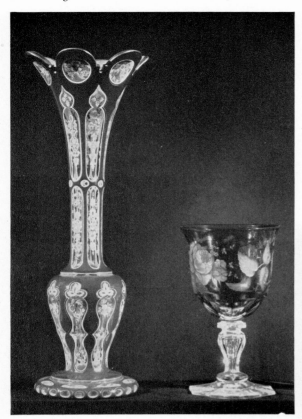

PLATE 62A. A cased-glass vase with painted decoration, about 1848; and a goblet with cased bowl and with engraving designed by W. J. Muckley, said to have been shown in the 1851 Exhibition. Both made by W. H., B. and J. Richardson. Ht 16 in. and 7¾ in. *Borough of Stourbridge Glass Collection.*

PLATE 62B. Engraved jug, shown at the 1851 Exhibition by J. G. Green, London. Ht 13¼ in. *Victoria and Albert Museum.*

PLATE 63A. Painted water-carafe, designed by Richard Redgrave for Henry Cole's "Summerly's Art Manufactures" and made by J. F. Christy, Lambeth, *c.* 1847. Ht 10¼ in. *Victoria and Albert Museum.*

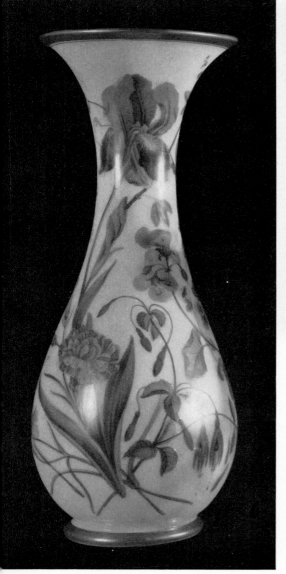

PLATE 63B. Painted opal vase, made by W. H., B. and J. Richardson, Stourbridge, *c.* 1851. Ht 17⅜ in. *Borough of Stourbridge Glass Collection.*

PLATE 64A. Comport, dish and decanter of cut crystal, made by W. H., B. and J. Richardson and said to have been shown at the 1851 Exhibition. Ht 5⅜ in., 2⅛ in. and 14¾ in. *Borough of Stourbridge Glass Collection (comport) and Mrs E. Worrall.*

PLATE 64B. Engraved wine glasses, with plain stem and with colour-threaded and convoluted stem, made by George Bacchus and Sons, Birmingham, about the early fifties. Ht 4½ in. and 5 in. *Victoria and Albert Museum.*